Microsoft
Money 98
At a Glance

Microsoft Press

Published by **Microsoft Press**
A Division of Microsoft Corporation
One Microsoft Way
Redmond, Washington 98052-6399

Library of Congress Cataloging-in-Publication Data
Nelson, Stephen L., 1959-
    Microsoft Money 98 At a Glance / Stephen L. Nelson
        p.   cm
    Includes index.
    ISBN 1-57231-639-X
    1. Microsoft Money. 2. Financial, Personal--Computer programs.
 3. Investments--Computer programs.   I. Title.
 HG179.N426147 1997
 332.024'00285'5369--dc21

                                               97-29787
                                               CIP

Printed and bound in the United States of America.

1 2 3 4 5 6 7 8 9   QEQE   2 1 0 9 8 7

Distributed to the book trade in Canada by Macmillan of Canada, a division of Canada Publishing Corporation.

A CIP catalogue record for this book is available from the British Library.

Microsoft Press books are available through booksellers and distributors worldwide. For further information about international editions, contact your local Microsoft Corporation office. Or contact Microsoft Press International directly at fax (206) 936-7329.

For Stephen L. Nelson, Inc.
Writers: **Steve Nelson, Kaarin Dolliver**
Editor: **Paula Thurman**
Technical Editor: **Beth Shannon**

For Microsoft Press
Acquisitions Editor: **Susanne Freet**
Project Editor: **Lucinda Rowley**

Contents

*How do I import
a Quicken file?*

see page 9

Favorite Account Balances

▶ US Bank Checking
▶ US Bank Savings

Add an account to
your Favorites list
see page 17

Create a chart from a report
see page 52

*How do I add
tax-deduction
categories to my
Categories List?*

see page 82

How can I use Money to compare mortgages?

see page 93

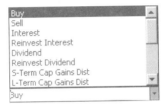

Describe the investments
in your portfolio
see page 104

Type

- ○ Family members
- ⊙ Properties
- ○ Projects
- ○ Hobbies

Create classifications to track
real estate income and
expenses by property
see page 129

*How do I add
downloaded
transactions
to my account
register?*

see page 147

Mark a customer's
invoice as paid
see pages 164–165

*How do I
track payroll
liabilities with
Money?*

see page 168

About This Book

Microsoft *Money 98 At a Glance* is for anyone who wants to exploit the power of Microsoft's personal finance manager, Money 98. You'll find this book to be a straightforward, easy-to-read reference tool. Based on the premise that it's tough to make "smart" decisions about money, this book's purpose is to help you use your computer as a tool to better organize and manage your financial affairs.

No Computerese!

Let's face it—when there's a task you don't know how to do but you need to get it done in a hurry, or when you're stuck in the middle of a task and can't figure out what to do next, there's nothing more frustrating than having to read page after page of technical background material. You want the information you need—nothing more, nothing less—and you want it now! *And* it should be easy to find and understand.

That's what this book is all about. It's written in plain English—no technical jargon and no computerese. There's no single task in the book that takes more than two pages. (And most take a page or less.) Just look up the task in the index or the table of contents, turn to the page, and there's the information, laid out step by step and accompanied by a graphic image or two to add visual clarity. You don't get bogged down by the whys and wherefores: just follow the steps, look at the illustrations, and get your work done with a minimum of hassle.

Occasionally you might have to turn to another page if the procedure you're working on has a "See Also" in the left column. That's because there's a lot of overlap among tasks, and I didn't want to keep repeating myself. I've also scattered some useful tips here and there, and thrown in a "Try This" once in a while, but by and large I've tried to remain true to the heart and soul of the book, which is that the information you need should be available to you at a glance.

Useful Tasks...

Whether you use Money to track several investment portfolios or simply to help keep your checkbook, I've tried to pack this book with procedures for everything that you might want to do, from the simplest tasks to some of the more esoteric ones.

...And the Easiest Way To Do Them

Another thing I've tried to do in *Microsoft Money* 98 *At a Glance* is to find and document the easiest way to accomplish a task. Like most software programs, Money often provides a multitude of methods to accomplish a single end result, which can be daunting or delightful, depending on the way you like to work. If you tend to stick with one favorite and familiar approach, the methods described in this book are the way to go. If you like trying out alternative techniques, go ahead! The intuitiveness of Money invites exploration, and you're likely to discover ways of doing things that you think are easier or that you like better than mine. If you do, that's great! It's exactly what the designers of Money had in mind when they provided so many alternatives.

A Quick Overview

This book isn't meant to be read in any particular order. It's designed so that you can jump in, get the information you need, and then close the book and keep it near your computer until the next time you need to know how to get something done. But that doesn't mean I scattered the information about with wild abandon. If you were to read the book from front to back, you'd find a logical progression from the simple tasks to the more complex ones. Here's a quick overview.

You'll probably turn first to Section 2. It introduces Money, explains how you can begin using Money, and describes some Money basics that you want to know as you begin exploring this useful tool.

If you're brand new to accounting software, you'll want to review Sections 3 and 4, which describe everything you need to know about using Money's account registers to keep track of your basic accounts. Section 3 describes how you use Money to keep track of your bank accounts, and Section 4 describes how you use Money to monitor credit card accounts.

Everyone should read Sections 5 and 6, which contain a wealth of information useful to all levels of Money users. Section 5 explains Money's Report and Chart feature. It talks in depth about the different kinds of reports and charts you can create, and why and when you would want to create some of the more common reports. Section 6 describes how you use the tools in Money 98 Financial Suite to build a budget, plan for the future, and track income and deductions for taxes.

Sections 7, 8, and 9 describe different types of specialized accounts you might want to create and use if you have loans, liabilities, investments, or assets you want Money to help you track. Section 7 describes how you can use Money to track your assets and liabilities. It goes through the different kinds of transactions you make in loan and liability accounts and provides several tips and strategies for getting out of debt. Sections 8 and 9 describe how you can use Money to track your investments. Section 8 deals with mutual funds, stocks, and bonds, and Section 9 deals with passive and active real estate investments.

If you have an Internet connection, you'll definitely want to review Section 10, which describes how you can use Money to bank, make electronic payments, and invest online. This section discusses how to set up online banking and bill payment services with participating banks, and also discusses where you can find financial advice on the Internet.

The remaining section of this book delves into a more advanced topic. It discusses how you can use Money to keep track of small business finances. You'll only need to read this section if you have a small business and want to use Money to help with your business accounting. This section describes such things as invoicing, accounts receivable accounting, and preparing payroll.

Some Final Words

Let me close this introductory section with some final comments—comments, I hope, that you'll find helpful and encouraging as you use this book and learn Money:

Whatever you *want* to do, this book helps you get it done.

This book helps you discover how to do things you *didn't* know you wanted to do.

And, finally, this book helps you *enjoy* using Money.

I hope you'll have as much fun using *Microsoft Money 98 At a Glance* as I did writing it. The best way to learn is by *doing*, and that's what you'll get from this book.

Jump right in!

2

The Basics of Money

Getting started with Microsoft Money is really very easy because you don't need much prior computer knowledge to begin using the program. But that much said, let me suggest that you'll benefit by having a little friendly help starting out and navigating your way through Money for the first time. This way, you'll get up and running more quickly, you'll quickly get the feel for Money's general organization, and you won't make simple mistakes that cause you to waste time later or miss out on some neat benefit.

Don't worry if you're not an expert on personal finance, budgeting, or investments. Of course it helps if you know something about these topics, but this knowledge isn't required to make good use of Money. As a matter of fact, as you read through this book or flip to a certain page for help with a task, you are almost certain to find a financial tip or two or a definition of a term to help you out.

Getting Started with Money

To use Money, of course, you first need to install it. If you're not sure whether or not Money is installed, just click the Start button and then choose Programs. If you see Microsoft Money listed, the program is already installed. If Money isn't already installed, you can install it in the same way that you install any other Windows-based application.

Shortcut to
Msmoney.exe

Install Money

1 Click the Start button, and choose Settings.

2 Choose the Control Panel command. Windows displays the Control Panel window.

3 Double-click the Add/Remove Programs icon. Windows displays the Add/Remove Programs Properties dialog box.

4 Click the Install/Uninstall tab in the Add/Remove Programs Properties dialog box, if it isn't already showing.

5 Insert the first Money disk in your floppy disk drive, or insert the Money CD-ROM in your CD-ROM drive.

6 Click the Install button.

7 Follow the instructions on the screen and press Enter when you are requested to. If you install Money from floppy disks, you'll be prompted to replace floppy disks one or two times during the installation.

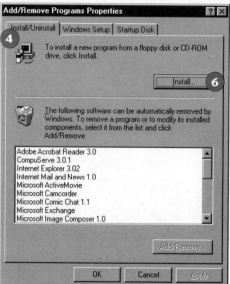

You can install and run both the standard version of Money 98 and Money 98 Financial Suite in the same way.

Run Money

1 Click the Start button.

2 Choose Programs.

3 Choose the Programs menu's Microsoft Money command.

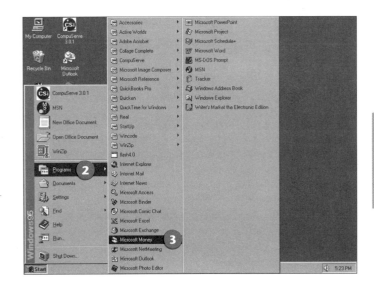

Creating and Opening Money Files

When you run Money, the first screen you'll see is the Home screen. If you've just installed Money, you can click where it says Take A Tour Of Money98 if you want to preview Money 98's features. At this point, you are also ready to begin setting up accounts in the file that Money has created for you, or you can open an existing account, create another new account, or import an account from Quicken.

TIP

If you need to open a backup copy of your Money file (because your original was damaged or destroyed), choose the File menu's Restore Backup command.

Open a Money File

1. Choose the File menu's Open command to display the Open dialog box.

2. Click the down arrow in the Look In drop-down list box, and locate the drive or folder in which your Money file is stored.

3. Double-click the Money file when you find it.

Create a Money File

1. Choose the File menu's New command.

2. Enter a name for the file in the File Name text box, and click OK.

3. Money creates the new file and displays the Money Home screen.

4. Click where it says Set Up Your Accounts to begin creating accounts within the Money file.

TIP

You need to create a separate Money file for each business whose finances you want to track using Money. It is also a good idea to let older children have their own separate Money files so that they can learn to track their accounts and spending and watch their savings grow.

TIP

By default, Money saves the Money files you create in the Microsoft Money subfolder of the Programs Files folder.

TIP

If you have an existing file open when you tell Money that you want to create a new file, Money prompts you to back up the open file. This is because Money can display only one file at a time. Click Back Up, and if necessary, click Yes to replace the existing backup copy or click Browse to store the backed up copy in a different location.

Import a File from Quicken

1 Choose the File menu's Open command to display the Open dialog box.

2 Select Quicken Files from the Files Of Type drop-down list box.

3 Click the down arrow in the Look In drop-down list box, and locate the drive and folder in which your Quicken file is stored. The default folder for your Quicken files is the Quickenw folder.

4 Double-click the Quicken file when you find it to start the Converter Wizard for Quicken, and click Next to continue.

5 Money suggests a name and storage location for the new Money file it will create from your Quicken file. You can change the name if you want, but keep the file stored wherever Money suggests and click Next to begin converting the files.

6 Click Finish.

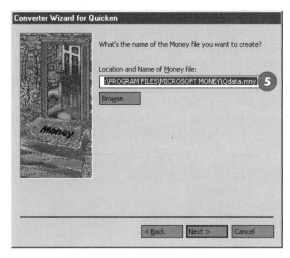

The Money Home Screen

Use the navigation bar at the top of every window to navigate your way through Money.

Click here to return to the Money Home screen.

Click once here to display an account register, or click twice to view all of your accounts in the Account Manager.

Click here to move backward through the windows you've recently visited.

Click here to browse through articles on financial topics in Money 98 Financial Suite.

Money 98 Financial Suite's Advisor FYI looks at the transactions you've entered in your accounts and provides advice.

Click here to go to the account registers of your favorite accounts.

Getting Help in Money

If you have questions about how a Microsoft Money command works, you can access help in several different ways.

Get Help with Screen Elements

1 Right-click the text box or button you need help with.

2 Choose the shortcut menu's What's This command.

Get Help with a Task

1 Choose the Help menu's Help Topics command.

2 Click one of the Help dialog box's tabs to search through Help topics.

◆ Click the Contents tab to see the topics organized in folders like a table of contents.

◆ Click the Find tab to search the Help topics for a specific word or phrase.

Type the name of the task you need help with here.

Double-click a task to display the help file on that task.

Archiving Money Files

Over time you will probably find that your accounts fill up quickly with dozens of transactions. After a year or so, you may want to rid your Money file of old transactions to make your accounts quicker and easier to work with. To do this, you create an archive file by removing selected transactions from selected accounts. By archiving your Money file, you still maintain old records, you just move them to another file to streamline your current Money file.

Archive a Money File

1 Choose the File menu's Archive command.

2 Enter the cut-off date before which you want specified transactions removed.

3 Click OK.

4 Enter a name for the archive file or accept the default name. Do not change the file type or the storage location that Money suggests.

5 Click OK.

6 Tell Money which types of files you want removed from each of your Money accounts by selecting options for each account and clicking OK to proceed to the next account.

Finishing a Money Session

As soon as you start using Money, you'll want to begin backing up the financial information you collect. This ensures that you have a separate copy of your financial records in case the original copies are destroyed or corrupted.

Back Up a Money File

1 Choose the File menu's Backup command to display the Back Up dialog box.

2 Click the Browse button.

3 Click the down arrow in the Save In drop-down list box, and select the floppy drive where you want your files backed up. (This is probably the a or b drive.)

4 Accept Money's suggested filename, and click OK.

5 If you have previously backed up to the same disk, click OK when Money asks if it can overwrite the file.

Exit Money

1 Choose the File menu's Exit command.

Keeping Your Checkbook

3

At its core, Microsoft Money is a computerized checkbook. Instead of keeping track of your checks and deposits in a paper register, you use an on-screen register. You get several very important benefits from computerizing your checkbook records:

◆ Your computer calculates your account balances so that as long as you enter the correct numbers, your account balance is correct.

◆ You can describe checks as falling into specific income and expense categories. That way, you can find out how much you spend in a certain category with just a couple of mouse clicks.

◆ You can reconcile your account in roughly two minutes.

◆ You can print checks or transmit payments electronically, which makes paying bills much easier and much quicker.

Setting Up Bank Accounts

To use Money, you set up an account for each bank account you want to track. Then you open the register and record the checks you write and the deposits you make for each account. Money doesn't change the way you record checks and deposits; it simply provides an on-screen form for you to use in place of the paper register that the bank gives you when you open a new account.

US Bank
Checking

SEE ALSO

For information on setting up accounts for online services, see "Setting Up Online Services" in Section 10.

TIP

Money asks you whether you want to set up online services only if you entered the name of your bank in step 2.

Create an Account

1 Click Accounts on the navigation bar once or twice to display the Account Manager, and then click the New Account button.

2 Enter the name of your bank or select it from the drop-down list, and click Next.

3 Select either Checking, Savings, or Bank from the list, and click Next.

4 Type a name for your account or accept the default Money provides, and click Next.

5 Select a category that describes the account, and click Next.

6 Enter the account number if you know it, and click Next.

7 Enter the ending balance from your last bank statement, and click Next.

8 If you don't want to set up any more accounts for the moment, click the I Have No Other Accounts At This Bank option button, and click Next.

9 Money asks you whether you want to find out about online services at your bank. Click the No, Not Now option button.

10 Click Finish.

TRY THIS

To open an account from the Account Manager, double-click the icon for the account you want to open.

Open an Account Register

1. Click Accounts on the navigation bar.

2. To move to the register of a different account, click the down arrow on the Accounts bar.

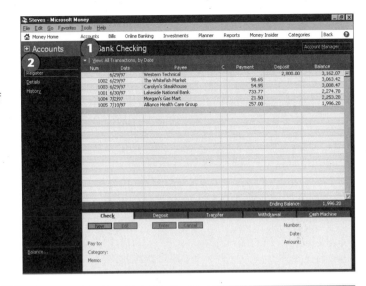

TIP

If you use an account frequently, it makes sense to check it as a favorite so that you can access it quickly. If you check an account as a favorite, it will appear at the top of the Go menu and on the Money Home screen.

Add an Account to Your Favorites List

1. With the account's register displayed, click Details.

2. Check the Favorite Account box.

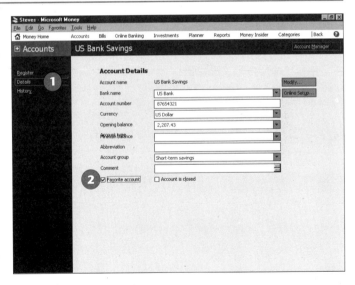

Storing Additional Account Information

You can easily store additional information about all the different kinds of accounts you create. You can store notes about interest rates, minimum balance requirements, and transaction fees.

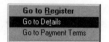

TIP

You can also use the Account Details window to edit the account setup. For example, you can edit the name of the account or the opening balance.

Store Information About Your Bank Account

1. Display the account register.

2. Click Details, and Money displays the Account Details window for the account.

3. Enter the minimum balance in the Minimum Balance field.

4. Use the Comment field to write notes to yourself, such as a reminder about fees you want to avoid.

Recording Income

When you enter transactions in a register, you use the transaction forms at the bottom of the Account Register window. Click the tab you want to use, and then describe the deposit or withdrawal by filling in the fields. To move between the fields, press the Tab key or click the mouse on the field you want to fill in. When you finish, click the Enter button. Money records your transaction and recalculates the balance.

TIP

You don't need to record an income transaction for interest earned on your bank account. You can do this when you reconcile the account.

SEE ALSO

For more information about entering recurring deposits, see page 29.

SEE ALSO

For more information on splitting transactions between categories, see page 26.

Record a Deposit

1. In the bank account's register, click the Deposit tab, and if necessary, click New.

2. Optionally, enter a deposit number or check number in the Number field.

3. Enter the deposit date.

4. Enter the name of the person or business that is paying you.

5. Enter the amount of the deposit.

6. Click the down arrow in the Category field, and select an income category that describes the deposit.

7. Enter a memo for the deposit.

8. Click Enter.

Using the Paycheck Wizard

As you well know, a certain amount of your paycheck is deducted right off the top of your earnings each and every time your employer pays you. Even though this money never actually makes it into your hands, Money can help you keep track of these deductions. Money can help you monitor how much you pay in federal, state, and local income taxes, how much you are paying for health insurance, and how much you put in employer 401K plans.

Record a Paycheck

1 In the bank account's register, click the Deposit tab, and if necessary, click New.

2 Enter the paycheck number in the Number field.

3 Enter the deposit date.

4 Enter the name of your employer in the From field.

5 Enter the word Paycheck in the Category field to launch the Paycheck Wizard.

6 If this is the first time you are entering a paycheck, Money asks you a few questions to set up the Paycheck Wizard to meet your needs. Answer the questions, and click Next to move on. Click Finish to begin entering your first paycheck.

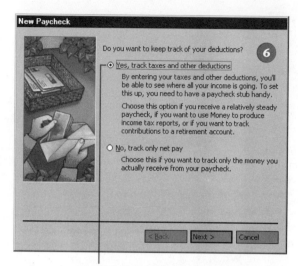

Click this option button to have Money help you track your deductions.

Employer retirement accounts. *If you have a tax-deferred retirement account through your employer, you can set up a Money account for it in the Paycheck Wizard by typing a name for the retirement account when Money asks. A retirement account works the same way as a regular investment account, so refer to Section 8 for more information about working with a retirement account.*

7 Enter the deduction amounts in the appropriate fields that Money has set up for you.

8 Click Done, and the Paycheck Wizard enters the paycheck amount in the Amount field.

9 Enter a memo (such as the pay period or job) in the Memo field.

10 Click Enter to record the paycheck.

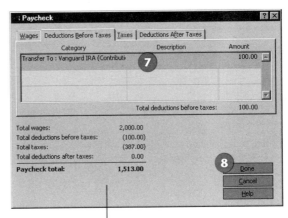

The Paycheck Wizard categorizes the deductions and displays a paycheck summary.

Recording Expenses

Recording expenses works in much the same way as recording income. The only real difference is which tab of the bank account's transaction form you use.

SEE ALSO

If a check falls into more than one category, see "Splitting Transactions" on page 26.

TIP

If you can't find a category that adequately describes an income or expense, you can create a new category by entering it in the Category box. When you click Enter, Money displays a dialog box that asks you to name and describe the category. You can also create subcategories within categories in the same way.

Record a Check

1. In the bank account's register, click the Check tab, and if necessary, click New.

2. Enter the check number, or type *P* for Print.

3. Enter the check date.

4. Enter the name of the person or business you're paying.

5. Enter the check amount.

6. Click the down arrow in the Category field, and select an expense category that describes the check.

7. Click Enter to record the check.

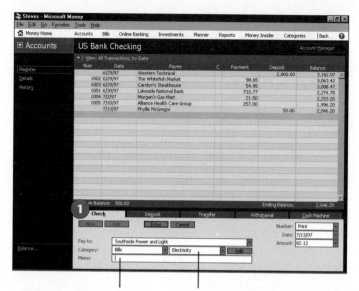

Enter a memo for the check to help you remember it.

Select a subcategory from the list if you want to describe your spending in that category more specifically.

TIP

If you withdraw money in another currency, you can use Money's Currency Converter calculator to convert foreign currency amounts back into dollars. Just press F8 in the Amount field, and fill out the Currency Converter dialog box with the current exchange rate.

Record an ATM Withdrawal

1 In the bank account's register, click the Cash Machine tab, and if necessary, click New.

2 Enter the withdrawal date.

3 Enter the withdrawal amount.

4 Categorize the cash withdrawal using the Category fields or the Split button.

5 Enter a memo to describe the withdrawal.

6 Click Enter to record the withdrawal.

Timesaving Tips for Entering Transactions

◆ You can enter transactions directly in the register without using transaction forms (the tabs at the bottom of the Account Register window) by clicking the View down arrow and choosing Transaction Forms to deselect it.

◆ AutoComplete remembers every transaction you make, and if it thinks it recognizes a payee name as you're typing, it will fill in the rest of the name for you so that you don't have to keep typing. If AutoComplete is correct, just press the Tab key to have it fill out the rest of the check for you. (You can change the check amount or any of the other fields if you need to.) If you don't want to accept the match AutoComplete finds, just continue typing.

◆ If you want to enter a memo to yourself that you don't want to appear on a printed check or an online payment, just put the memo inside curly brackets ({}) in the Pay To field.

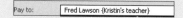

◆ To enter today's date in the Date field, type Ctrl+D. Type a plus sign (+) to go to the next day or a minus sign (-) to go to the previous day.

◆ AutoComplete by default enters the next check number if you tell it you want to record another check. Click the plus sign (+) to go to the following number or the minus sign (-) to go to the previous number.

◆ Click the down arrow in the Date field to enter a date using the Calendar. Click the arrows at the sides of the month to go forward or backward through the months to find a date; then click the date to enter it in the Date field.

◆ If you need to add, subtract, multiply, or divide numbers to get a deposit or withdrawal amount, click the down arrow beside the Amount field to display the calculator. Click the numbers and operators and then click = to calculate the amount.

Recording Transfers

There's a good chance that you have both a checking account and a savings account. If this is the case, you should know how to record one other type of bank account transaction, an account transfer. This works pretty much like you'd expect: you need to identify the accounts you're moving money between, the date of the transfer, and the amount of the transfer.

US Bank Checking   US Bank Savings

SEE ALSO

For more information about transferring money electronically with online banking, see page 148.

Record a Transfer

1. Click the Transfer tab, and if necessary, click New.

2. Enter the name of the account you're moving money from.

3. Enter the transfer date.

4. Enter the name of the account you're moving money to.

5. Enter the transfer amount.

6. Leave the Pay To field empty.

7. Optionally, enter a memo in the Memo field.

8. Click Enter to record the transfer and recalculate the balance for both accounts.

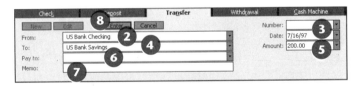

Splitting Transactions

Especially if you're a frequent "one-stop shopper," you'll find that oftentimes a single check you write falls into several categories. Fortunately, Money lets you split transactions into different categories. For example, maybe you wrote a check to a local grocery store, but the check didn't buy just one thing. You bought some groceries. You had a drug prescription filled. And you bought some flowers for a friend's birthday. Money makes it easy to record this check in three spending categories.

TIP

You can add a new category or subcategory to the categories list by typing it in the Category or Subcategory box.

Split a Transaction

1 Click the Split button. Money displays the Split Transaction dialog box.

2 Enter the first category on the first line.

3 Optionally, select a subcategory for that purchase or income.

4 Optionally, enter a memo to describe the first spending category. For example, you might want to list exactly what you bought.

5 Enter the amount spent or received in the first category in the Amount field.

6 Repeat steps 3 through 5 on the second and subsequent lines for each spending category and subcategory.

7 Click Done when you finish. Money closes the Split Transaction dialog box and returns you to the Account Register Transaction form so that you can continue filling out your transaction.

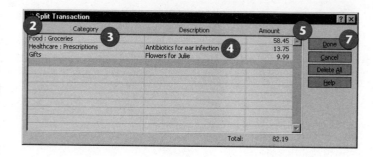

Fixing Errors

It is easy to fix mistakes you happen to make while entering checks, deposits, and account transfers. Deleting or voiding a transaction is even simpler.

Edit a Transaction

1 Double-click the transaction you want to edit.

2 Click the field you want to edit

3 Enter your correction, and click Enter.

Delete a Transaction

1 Select the transaction you want to delete.

2 Choose the Edit menu's Delete command.

3 Confirm that you want to delete the transaction by clicking Yes.

Void a Check

1 Go to the account register.

2 Select the check you want to void.

3 Choose the Edit menu's Mark As Void command.

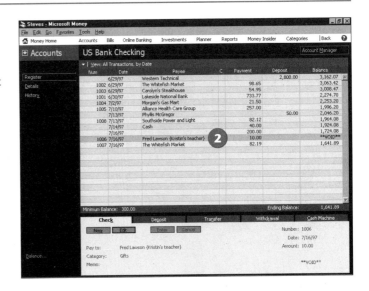

Entering Recurring Transactions

You can use Money's Payment Calendar to help keep track of recurring transactions, such as direct deposit paychecks and automatic mortgage or insurance payments. You can also use it to keep track of recurring bills, such as monthly utility bills. Money's Payment Reminder reminds you when these bills are due.

TIP

When the recurring payment approaches. *When a payment is 10 days away from being due, you will get a Reminder in the Money Home screen. Go to the Bills area and confirm that you have enough money in your account to pay the bill by checking in the New Balance After Entering column. Then check the boxes of the transactions you want to enter in your Account Register, and click Enter. Click Enter again to record the transactions.*

Add a Recurring Payment

1. Click Bills on the navigation bar.

2. Click the New Bill button.

3. Click the Bill option button, and click Next twice.

4. Click the down arrow in the Frequency field, and select how often the payment is made.

5. Click the down arrow in the Account field, and select the account you signed permission to use for paying the bill.

6. Enter the Date for the first payment.

7. Enter the name of the person or business you are paying.

8. Enter the amount of the payment.

9. Categorize the payment.

10. Click OK to add the payment to the Payment Calendar.

Click the arrows on the side of the calendar on the Bills bar to move forward or backward a month and see which recurring transactions will be due by that time.

Add a Recurring Deposit to the Payment Calendar

1 Click the New Bill button.

2 Click the Deposit option button, and click Next twice.

3 Click the down arrow in the Frequency field, and select how often the deposit is made.

4 Click the down arrow in the Account field, and select the account you set up to accept the deposit.

5 Enter the Date for the first deposit.

6 Enter the name of the person or business paying you.

7 Enter the amount of the deposit.

8 Categorize the deposit.

9 Click OK to add the deposit to the Payment Calendar.

Create New Recurring Payment

Choose the type of Recurring Payment to create:

○ Bill
Such as telephone bill, rent payment.

⊙ Deposit **2**
Such as paycheck deposit, or other regular income.

○ Transfer
Such as transfers from checking to savings.

○ Investment Purchase
Such as regular contributions to a mutual fund.

< Back | Next > | Cancel

Edit Scheduled Deposit

Frequency: Monthly **3**   Entry method: Manual E... **9** OK / Cancel

Deposit
Account: US Bank Checking **4**   Number: **5**
From: Western Technical **6**   Date: 7/30/97
Category: Wages & Salary | Net Pay | Split **8**   Amount: 2,800.00 **7**
Memo:

3

Finding Lost Transactions

Although Money can't help you much in proving that you did indeed make that payment that got lost in the mail, it can give you a little peace of mind if you can't remember whether or when or how much you paid someone.

TIP

By default, Money searches through all of your accounts. This helps you find transactions you mistakenly entered in the wrong account. If you want to limit your search to particular accounts, however, use the Account tab to specify the accounts you want to search.

TIP

If you want to conduct a new search, click New Search to clear your previous search.

Search for Transactions by Category

1 Choose the Tools menu's Find command and the Find submenu's Transactions command.

2 Click the Categories tab.

3 Select one of the Categories options.

- ◆ Click Selected Categories to find transactions in a small number of categories.

- ◆ Click Income Categories to find transactions in all or most income categories.

- ◆ Click Expense Categories to find transactions in all or most expense categories.

4 Select the categories you want to include or exclude from the search list by clicking them.

5 Click Find to find all the transactions in the categories you selected.

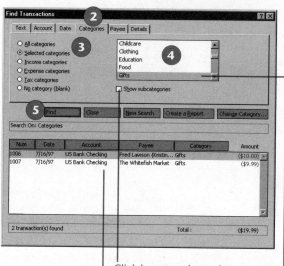

Click here to select subcategories to include in your search.

Money searches for the categories highlighted in this list.

If Money finds any matches to your search, it will list them here. Double-click a transaction to edit it.

Search for Transactions by Payee

1 Choose the Tools menu's Find command and the Find submenu's Transactions command.

2 Click the Payee tab.

3 Click the Selected Payees option button, and select the payee or payees from the list.

4 Click Find.

Money lists all of the search criteria you've specified on the different tabs here.

Narrow Your Search

1 Choose the Tools menu's Find command and the Find submenu's Transactions command.

2 Click the Details tab.

3 Specify the search criteria.

◆ Click the down arrow in the Transaction Type field to select a type of transaction, such as deposit or withdrawal.

◆ Click the down arrow in the Status field to select reconciled or unreconciled transactions.

4 Click Find.

Use the Number fields to search for checks within certain ranges.

Use the Amount fields to search for transactions within a range of amounts.

TIP

Use the Date tab to search for transactions recorded on a certain date or within a specific range of dates.

TIP

Use the Text tab if you want to search transactions for a word or phrase. This is especially useful if you need to find a transaction based on what you wrote in the memo field.

Printing Checks

You don't need to print your checks with Money, but many users do. The idea is that you save time—and produce neater check forms—by doing so. When you choose to print checks with Money, Money takes the information that you enter when you record your checks and uses that information to print your checks.

Print a Check

1 Display the checking account register.

2 Click Print Checks on the Accounts bar. (This button appears only after you've described a check you want to print.)

3 Select the check form you have, and click Next.

4 If you want to print only some of the checks, click the Selected Checks option button.

5 If you specified that you wanted to print only selected checks, Money displays the Select Checks dialog box. Click the computer checks you want to print, and then click OK to close the Select Checks dialog box.

Preventing check forgery.
It's a good idea to carefully sign your checks using a signature that isn't easily duplicated. Signatures that consist of just a wavy line and some squiggles are more easily forged. Also remember to write the word "VOID" in large letters across the face of any check that is incorrectly printed or written.

If you're unsure about which way to load the check forms in your printer, test it out by writing the words Left *and* Right *on a blank piece of paper and then printing a dummy check on this paper. You might even want to keep this dummy check as a reference.*

6 Look at the preprinted number of your first check form, and enter this number in the Number Of First Check In Printer field.

7 Load the appropriate number of checks in your printer, and click Print. Money prints your computer checks.

8 If the computer checks printed correctly, click Finish. If they didn't, click Reprint.

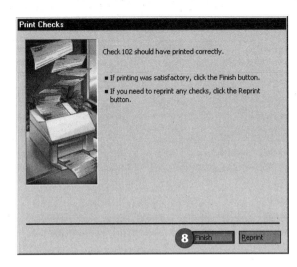

Print Checks

Check 102 should have printed correctly.

- If printing was satisfactory, click the Finish button.
- If you need to reprint any checks, click the Reprint button.

8 Finish | Reprint

3

Reconciling Bank Accounts

Let's face it. One of the most tedious tasks in keeping a checking account is balancing, or reconciling, the account. Yet it's extremely important to do so. By comparing your records with the bank's, you can catch errors you've made in recording transactions and usually catch errors made by the bank as well. Only by regularly balancing an account can you protect yourself against problems such as forgery and embezzlement.

Reconcile a Bank Account

1 Display the account register for the bank account you want to reconcile.

2 Click Balance on the Accounts bar. Money displays an introductory Balance dialog box. Click Next.

3 In the next dialog box, enter the bank statement ending date in the Statement Date field.

4 Enter the bank statement opening, or starting, balance in the Starting Balance field.

5 Enter the bank statement closing, or ending, balance in the Ending Balance field.

6 If your bank statement shows a monthly service charge, use the Service Charge and Category fields to describe this expense.

7 If your bank statement shows any interest income, use the Interest Earned and Category fields to describe this income.

8 After you've completed the Balance dialog box, click Next.

Balance US Bank Checking

Enter the following information from your statement:

Statement date: 7/16/97 **3**

Starting balance: 362.07 **4**

Ending balance: 1,640.39 **5**

If applicable, also enter the following:

Service charge: 1.50 **6**

Category: Bank Charge | Service Char

Interest earned: **7**

Category: Investment 1 | Interest

8 Next > | Cancel

9 Mark the checks and deposits that have cleared the bank.

◆ Click in the C (for cleared) column for all checks and withdrawals that show on your bank statement. When you do, Money places a C in this column to signal that these transactions have cleared the bank

◆ Click in the C (for cleared) column for all deposits that show on your bank statement. When you do, Money places a C in this column to signal that these transactions have cleared the bank

10 When the difference between the cleared balance and the bank statement balance equals zero, click Next. Money displays another dialog box congratulating you for balancing your account.

11 Click Finish. Money redisplays the account register in its usual format.

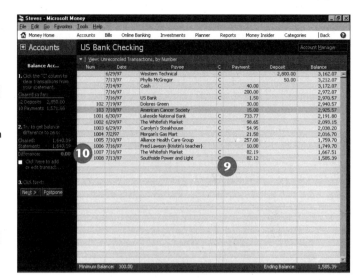

I Can't Get My Account to Balance

If, after you complete the step-by-step process described on the previous pages, the cleared balance still doesn't equal the statement balance, the problem probably lies in one of the following places:

- You made a mistake marking transactions as cleared.
- The register is missing one or more transactions.
- You or the bank recorded a transaction incorrectly.

If you find yourself in this situation, your best bet is first to be sure that your account register isn't missing a transaction. You can do this by checking that every transaction that appears on the bank statement also appears in the account register. I find, for example, that it's really easy to miss an automated teller machine (ATM) transaction or two. You can add a missing transaction directly in the Account Register window that shows when you're reconciling an account.

When you're sure that you've entered any missing transactions, verify that each transaction you recorded as "cleared" has really cleared. If you incorrectly marked an uncleared transaction as cleared, unmark it. If you accidentally left a cleared transaction marked as uncleared, by all means clear it.

Finally, compare the transaction amounts shown in your register with the transaction amounts shown on your bank statement. If you discover that you've entered one of your checks or deposits incorrectly, you can fix it by editing it in the list of unreconciled transactions. For example, you can change check or deposit information by clicking on the incorrect information and then editing or typing over the existing text or number.

Remember that in setting up your accounts, you need to begin with an accurate account balance, preferably a just-reconciled account balance. If you don't begin with an accurate balance, you might not be able to reconcile the account balance because your starting balance is wrong. In this case, there's not much you can do unless you want to go back to your old banking records and try to find the error or errors that made your starting account balance wrong. If you do find yourself in this situation, by the way, I suggest that you attempt to balance your bank account every month—and then give up once you can't go any further. (By clicking the Postpone button, Money saves your work and returns you to a regular view of the account register.)

This sounds lazy and perhaps crazy, but here's my logic. If you can't balance the account but the difference is the same every month—$41.35 in January, $41.35 in February, and $41.35 in March, for example—you'll know that the account won't balance because of errors you made at least as early as January. And in this case, I think it makes more sense to adjust the account balance so that your account does balance rather than waste any time looking for the error or errors that explain the mysterious $41.35. Money is, after all, supposed to make managing your finances less work, not more work.

To adjust the account balance, click Finish, even though Money still shows a difference between your records and the bank's. When Money displays the Balance Account dialog box, click the Automatically Adjust The Account Balance option button, use the Category boxes to categorize the adjustment, and click Next.

Two Notorious Bank Account Errors

Two types of bank account errors are notoriously difficult to catch, so let me tell you what they are and how you catch them.

- ◆ Transposing Numbers

    For example, say you enter a check as $21.34 when it really should have been entered as $23.14. You've entered the correct digits, but in the wrong order. This error is tough to catch because as you look through your checks and deposits, you see the transaction, see that it has all the right digits, but fail to notice the transposed 1 and 3.

- ◆ Entering a Check as a Deposit or a Deposit as a Check

    People make this error when they enter a transaction in the register but stick the amount in the wrong column. You can usually catch this error by marking your checks and other withdrawals as "cleared" in a batch and then marking your deposits as "cleared" in a batch.

Errors That Balancing Won't Catch

The main reason that you should balance bank accounts is to find errors you or the bank made in recording checks, deposits, and other transactions. But a reconciliation won't catch bookkeeping errors.

One such error is a transaction that you've forgotten to record in your account register and that hasn't yet cleared the bank. If the missing transaction is a check (and it most likely is a check, since you usually have more checks than deposits), you think you have more money in your checking account than you actually do. Unfortunately, the only way to avoid this error is to be diligent about recording your transactions.

Another type of error a reconciliation won't catch is a fictitious transaction you inadvertently recorded. Because the transaction is fictitious, it never shows up on a bank statement and is always listed as outstanding. Although the possibility of recording a fictitious transaction seems extreme, it can occur. You might, for example, record a weekly check to your daughter's piano teacher without actually printing the check.

Fictitious transactions have the opposite effect on your account balance than do uncleared transactions that you have forgotten to record: a fictitious check erroneously decreases the account balance, and a fictitious deposit erroneously increases the account balance. To prevent these errors, you simply need to be careful not to record transactions until they occur.

3

Closing Accounts

You probably don't close accounts very often, but if you do find yourself needing to close an account, you have two ways of telling Money that the account no longer exists. You can close the account so that you can still view its records and include its transactions in reports and charts, or you can delete the account and permanently remove all records of it.

Eastern City
Bank
Checking

TIP

A word of caution. *Deleting a Money account is a permanent action. If there are transactions in your account and Money asks you to confirm the delete, when you click Yes, the Money file is immediately deleted. You cannot recover it from the Recycle Bin. For this reason you will want to be especially careful when you delete accounts.*

Close an Account

1 Click Accounts on the navigation bar once or twice to display the Account Manager window.

2 Right-click the account you want to close.

3 Choose the shortcut menu's Account Is Closed command.

Delete an Account

1 Click Accounts on the navigation bar to display the Account Manager window.

2 Select the account you want to delete.

3 Click the Delete Account button.

4 If Money asks you to confirm the delete, click Yes.

4

Keeping Track of Credit Cards

Almost every time I hear of someone in financial trouble, the person's credit cards seem to be one of the main culprits. Credit cards are by their very nature problematic. You're carrying around a little piece of plastic that can be used at whim to respond to the calls of sophisticated advertising. And once you've got that brand-new credit card and a high starting credit limit, there aren't really any obstacles to keep you from purchasing leather shoes you can't afford or expensive stereo gear you don't need. Then, after you fall behind and begin carrying a balance, breaking out of the credit card trap becomes more and more difficult.

Microsoft Money can help you deal with your credit cards by letting you track the money you're spending with a credit card and the balance you've accumulated. Keeping these records produces a couple of interesting benefits. The most obvious benefit is that you know where you're spending money and how much you owe on your credit card. There's also a more subtle benefit to using Money to track your credit card spending: if you're someone who finds it easy to spend freely with credit cards, the simple act of recording each and every credit card purchase will very likely help you become more sensitive to the effects of saying, "Charge it."

Creating Credit Card Accounts

If you're already disciplined about how you use your credit card, you don't really need to set up a credit card account. You can just record checks to the credit card company in the same way that you record any other check, splitting the transaction for each of the items you bought over the month. If, on the other hand, you do carry a balance on your credit card or you're not disciplined about your credit card spending, you should definitely set up a credit card account.

Visa

Set Up a Credit Card Account

1 In the Account Manager window, click the New Account button. Money starts the New Account Wizard.

2 Enter the name of the bank or financial institution that issued your card, and click Next.

3 Select Credit Card from the list, and click Next.

4 Enter a name for the account (or accept the default), and click Next.

5 If you know your account number, enter it and click Next.

6 The wizard asks how much you owe on your credit card. Enter the amount listed in the Previous Balance portion of your current credit card statement, and click Next.

7 The wizard asks whether the card is a credit card or a charge card. Select the appropriate option, and click Next.

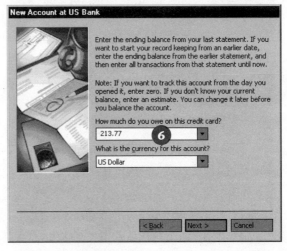

TIP

If you have Money 98 Financial Suite, click Money Insider on the navigation bar and then click the Credit & Debt hyperlink from the list on the right for more information on choosing credit cards and staying out of debt.

TRY THIS

If you aren't carrying a balance from your previous credit card statement, you can save yourself a little time by entering your balance as zero. This way, you do not need to record the amount of your last payment.

8 If you selected the credit card option, the wizard asks you about the card's interest rate. Enter the interest rate information, and click Next.

9 If your credit card has a credit limit, enter it in the field and then click Next.

10 Click the Keep Track Of Individual Credit Card Charges option button, and click Next.

11 The wizard asks if you want the credit card payments added to the list of recurring payments. If you do, check Yes and fill out the dialog box. Click Next.

12 Click the I Have No Other Accounts At This Bank option button, and click Next.

13 Select the No, Not Now option if Money asks whether you want to set up online services, and click Finish.

Enter the payment amount you'll probably have to make here.

Specify the date by which you'll next have to make a payment on the credit card balance here.

Indicate from which bank account you'll write a check for your credit card purchases here.

4

Recording Credit Card Purchases

To record a credit card purchase (or any other credit card transaction, for that matter), you display the account register of the credit card account. A credit card account register works the same way as a bank account register. To enter a credit card charge, you use the transaction form at the bottom of the Account Register window.

SEE ALSO

For more information about splitting transactions, see page 26.

TIP

Don't worry about recording interest and service charges. You record these charges when you reconcile your credit card account.

Record a Credit Card Purchase

1. Display the register of the credit card account.

2. Click the Charge tab, and if necessary, click New.

3. Enter the purchase date.

4. Enter the name of the person or business you paid.

5. Enter the amount of the purchase.

6. Click the down arrows in the Category fields to categorize the purchase, or click Split to split the transaction into more than one category.

7. Enter a memo in the Memo field.

8. Click Enter to record the transaction.

Recording Credit Card Credits

To record a credit card credit, such as you might receive when you return an item you bought with a credit card, you fill in the fields of the Credit tab the same way you fill in the fields of the Charge tab.

TIP

Although it might seem strange to do so, you want to record the credit using an expense category, namely the same one you used when you recorded the original purchase. This way, the balance in the category will reflect this refund.

Record a Credit Card Credit

1 Display the Account Register of the credit card account.

2 Click the Credit tab, and if necessary, click New.

3 Enter the credit date.

4 Enter the name of the person or business who refunded you.

5 Enter the amount of the credit.

6 Click the down arrows in the Category fields to categorize the credit.

7 Enter a memo in the Memo field to help you remember why your account was credited: what exactly you returned or whether the business made a mistake when they charged your account.

8 Click Enter to record the transaction.

Recording Credit Card Payments

To record a credit card payment, you record the check that you use to pay the credit card bill in the appropriate bank account register. For example, if I am going to pay my VISA bill by writing a check on a bank account that I named "US Bank Checking," I just write and record the check in the usual way. Then, rather than categorize the check, I transfer the money to the credit card account.

TIP
As with any transfer transaction in Money, you can record a credit card payment either in the register of the account receiving the money (in this case the credit card account) or in the register of the account giving the money (in this case the bank account).

Record a Credit Card Payment

1. Open either the credit card or bank account register.

2. Click the Transfer tab, and if necessary, click New.

3. Enter the check number.

4. Enter the transfer date.

5. Enter the name of the bank account you're writing a check on.

6. Enter the name of the credit card account you're paying.

7. Enter the amount of the credit card bill you're paying.

8. Enter the name of the credit card company.

9. Click Enter. Money records the credit card payment and recalculates the account balance for both accounts.

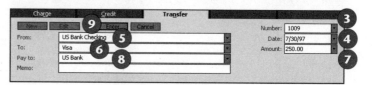

Tracking and Paying Off Credit Card Balances

Once you start using Money to monitor your credit card spending and your credit card balances, you'll find it much easier to be disciplined about the money you spend with credit cards. Money 98 Financial Suite also includes a tool to help you chart a plan for getting out of debt. If you've been carrying a balance and are curious about how long it would take to pay it down, you can use the Financial Suite's Debt Reduction Planner to find out.

Use the Debt Reduction Planner to Reduce Credit Card Debt

1 Click Planner on the navigation bar.

2 Click the Get Out Of Debt button, and then click Next to begin using the Debt Reduction Planner.

3 Select your credit card accounts from the list, and click the Move Into Plan button. Click Next.

4 Specify whether you want to base the plan on the amount you can pay each month or on the date by which you want to be out of debt.

5 Enter the amount you can pay each month or the date by which you want to be out of debt.

6 Specify any extra payments you can make.

7 Click Next to see your debt plan in a graph.

8 Click Next again to schedule payments for getting out of debt.

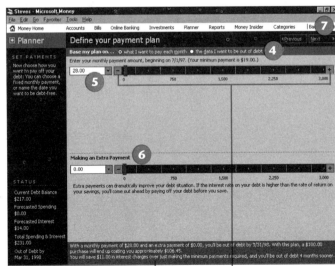

Money displays the results of your debt plan here and adjusts the values if you edit your input.

Click the plus or minus buttons to increase or decrease the amount by one dollar or one day.

4

Reconciling Credit Card Accounts

Reconciling a credit card account works in exactly the same way as reconciling a bank account. Before you begin, you need your last credit card statement and preferably all of your credit card receipts for the month.

Balanced on:	7/30/97
Balance...	

Reconcile a Credit Card Account

1. Display the account register for the credit card account you want to reconcile.

2. Click Balance on the Accounts bar.

3. Enter the credit card statement ending date in the Statement Date field.

4. Enter the previous balance from your credit card statement in the Total Amount You Owed Last Month field.

5. Enter the new balance from the credit card statement closing balance in the Total Amount You Owe This Month field.

6. If your credit card statement shows a service charge such as an annual fee, use the Service Charge and Category fields to describe this expense.

7. If your credit card statement shows any finance charges, use the Interest Charge and Category fields to describe this expense.

8. After you've completed the Balance Credit Card dialog box, click Next.

TIP

If Money alerts you that you have a balance remaining, you can click Pay Bill Now in the dialog box Money displays to enter a transfer transaction for the credit card payment.

9 Mark the purchases, credits, and payments that have cleared the account by clicking in the C (for cleared) column. When you do, Money places a C in this column to signal that these transactions have cleared the bank.

10 When the difference between the cleared balance and the credit card statement balance equals zero, click Next. Money displays another dialog box congratulating you for balancing your account.

11 Click the Finish button. Money redisplays the account register in its usual format.

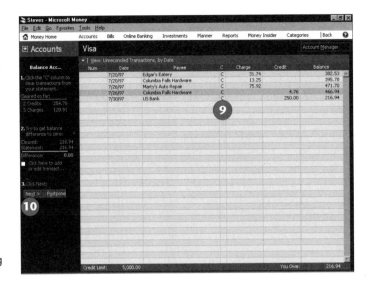

4

5

Creating Reports and Charts

Using Microsoft Money only for financial record-keeping delivers some benefits. Money, for example, calculates account balances automatically and accurately. It prints checks for you. And after you begin using Money, you'll discover that reconciling a bank account takes only a couple of minutes.

But the biggest benefit of using Money isn't that it allows you to do all of these things. The biggest benefit is that Money lets you sort and summarize the financial information you collect in many different ways. By using Money's reports, for example, you can see how much you're really spending on housing, groceries, work expenses, and so forth. You can easily track and tally tax deductions. And you can compare your actual income and expenses with whatever amounts you budgeted.

You can work with reports in several ways using Money. You can produce on-screen reports and customize them to show exactly what you want to see. You can also save your favorite reports to see how your spending habits change, and you can print and export reports to easily take them with you and show them to others.

Producing Reports

The makers of Money realized the importance of being able to visualize your finances, which is why they made the reports feature so quick and easy to use. Within a matter of minutes, you can create a detailed report of some aspect of your finances and customize it to show exactly what you want it to.

Report & Chart Gallery

TIP

To return to the Gallery of Reports and Charts after creating a report, click the Report & Chart Gallery button in the upper right corner of your screen.

Produce an On-Screen Report

1 Click Reports on the navigation bar.

2 Click a category on the Reports & Charts bar to see a list of reports and charts that summarize a particular aspect of your finances.

3 Select a specific report or chart from the list.

4 Click the Go To Report/ Chart button. Money produces the selected report or chart.

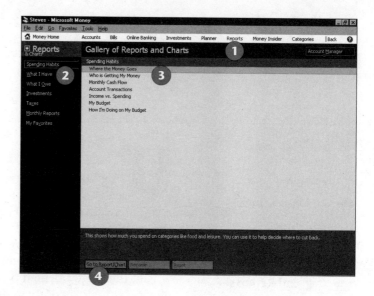

The Six Basic Report Categories

CATEGORY	DESCRIPTION	PURPOSE
Spending Habits	Summarizes transactions by payee or category and compares actual income and spending with budgeted income and spending	Allows you to see how you earn and spend your money, where you earn and spend your money, and how your actual earnings and expenditures compare to your plans
What I Have	Summarizes account balances at a point in time or over a period of time	Allows you to estimate your net worth and to see the estimated value of your assets and liabilities
What I Owe	Summarizes liability account balances and post-dated payment transactions	Allows you to gauge the magnitude of your debts and to plan repayment strategies
Investments	Summarizes investment account and transaction information	Allows you to assess the profitability of your investments and to perform year-end investment tax planning
Taxes	Summarizes tax-related transactions	Shows you what taxable income and tax deductions you'll report on your year-end tax return and allows you to perform year-end tax planning
Monthly Reports (Money 98 Financial Suite only)	Summarizes your spending habits, investment performance, budget, debt plan status, and Advisor FYI tips for the month	Allows you to view several aspects of your financial situation during any given month and compare the information with other months

5

Working with Reports

After you have created a report, you might want to turn that report into a chart so that you can easily see the information you are reporting on. With the click of a button, you can create a chart from a report, and then customize the chart to your liking. When you have your report or chart just the way you want it, you can save it so that you don't have to re-create it the next time.

TIP

You probably want to keep the Show In 3D check box clear because three-dimensional charts frequently distort data.

Create a Chart

1. Display or create the report from which you want to make a chart.

2. Click a Chart button.

3. Click Customize.

4. Use the Customize Chart dialog box to customize the chart.

   ◆ Click Bar to create a bar chart; then use the Bar Options buttons to tell Money whether you want your bars displayed side by side or in a single column.

   ◆ Click Line to create a line chart.

   ◆ Click Pie; then use the Pie Labels option buttons to tell Money how to label the pie chart.

5. Click Apply to preview the chart.

6. Click View to return to the Chart window.

Click the Reset button to return to the default chart.

Click the More Options button to specify the date range and accounts included in the chart.

Add a Report or Chart to the My Favorites List

1 Display or create the report or chart you want to add to your My Favorites list.

2 Click the Add To Favorites button.

3 In the Add To Favorites dialog box, enter a name for your customized report in the Report Name text box.

4 Click OK.

Producing Month-End and Year-End Reports

Money is capable of producing many different reports and charts. As a result, deciding which reports to produce can be a bit overwhelming. Fortunately, you can apply some good rules of thumb in this area. You should print out an Account Transactions report at the end of every month and file it with your bank statement and canceled checks. And you should print a Tax-Related Transaction report at the end of each year and store it with a copy of your tax return.

TIP

If you forget to back up your Money data, you can re-enter all the transactions from your Account Transactions reports to rebuild your financial records.

Create an Account Transactions Report

1. Click Spending Habits on the Reports & Charts bar.

2. Select Account Transactions from the Spending Habits list.

3. Click the Go to Report/Chart button.

4. Click Customize.

5. Click the down arrow in the Include Transactions From Account field, and select an account from the list.

6. Make sure that the All Transactions option is selected in the Include Transactions box.

7. Click the down arrow in the Dates field, and select Previous Month from the list.

8. Click View.

SEE ALSO

Section 6 describes in detail how Money 98 Financial Suite makes it easier to plan your income taxes and prepare your income tax returns.

TIP

To create a Tax-Related Transactions report to export to a tax preparation program, click Taxes on the Reports & Charts bar, and then select Tax Software Report from the Taxes list.

Create a Tax-Related Transactions Report

1. Click Taxes on the Reports & Charts bar.

2. Select Tax-Related Transactions from the Taxes list.

3. Click the Go To Report/ Chart button.

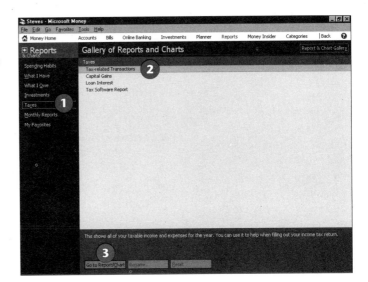

Customizing Reports

Since Money offers more than two dozen reports, you can usually find one that answers the questions you have. Nonetheless, Money gives you a rich set of customization options that you can use to change the appearance of reports. Changing the report time frame and the accounts included in the report are probably the most important and useful customizations you will make.

🗹 Account Transactions

TIP

Which options appear in the Customize Report dialog box depend on the report. Different reports have different customization options.

TIP

When you customize a report, it appears in the Gallery of Reports and Charts window with a notepad icon beside it.

Change the Report Time Frame

1. Display or create the report whose time frame you want to change.

2. Click Customize.

3. Click the down arrow in the Dates field, and select one of the date ranges.

4. Click View to close the Customize Report dialog box and update the report.

To keep your reports simple and easy to read, create a separate Account Transactions report for each of your accounts.

Change the Accounts Summarized

1 Display or create the report you want to customize.

2 Click Customize.

3 Click the down arrow in the Include Transactions From Account field, and select Multiple Accounts from the list. Money displays the Select Accounts dialog box. Initially, all of the listed accounts are selected.

4 Remove the accounts you don't want to include on the report by clicking them in the list.

5 Click OK to close the Select Accounts dialog box.

6 Click View to close the Customize Report dialog box and update the report. A notepad icon alerts you that this report has been customized.

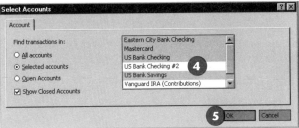

Formatting Reports

Once you have your report created and customized to show the information you want, you can also format it so that it is pleasing to the eye and can be easily read.

Change the Column Widths

1. Click Customize to display the Customize Report dialog box.

2. Click the Widths button to display the Set Report Column Widths dialog box.

3. Select one of the Width options.

4. Click OK.

5. Click View to return to your report.

Change the Font Style and Point Size

1. Click Customize to display the Customize Report dialog box.

2. Click the Fonts button to display the Select Font dialog box.

3. Select a font from the Font list box.

4. Select a font size from the Size list box.

5. Click OK to return to the Customize Report dialog box.

6. Click View to return to your report.

Printing Reports

Although on-screen reports are great, especially because you can create and manipulate them so quickly and easily, you may also want to have printed copies of your reports so that you can take them with you and show them to others—to your accountant, for instance.

Set Up Your Printer

1 Choose the File menu's Print Setup command.

2 Choose the Print Setup submenu's Report And Chart Setup command to display the Report And Chart Setup dialog box.

3 Select an Orientation option to specify whether Money should print pages in portrait or landscape orientation.

4 Click the Options button to display the printer's Properties dialog box, which you can use to change the paper tray, the print quality, and so forth. Click OK to return to the Report And Chart Setup dialog box.

5 Click OK.

Print a Report

1 Display the report or chart you want to print.

2 Choose the File menu's Print command to display the Print Report dialog box.

3 Select Print Range options to specify which part of your report you want to print.

4 Specify the number of copies to print in the Copies text box.

5 Click OK to print the report.

5

How Long to Keep Records

People throw around many different rules for retaining canceled checks, bank statements, copies of old tax returns, and other financial records. I suggest that you keep everything for seven years after you file a tax return. If you filed 1991's tax return in April of 1992, keep all of your 1991 tax return records until April of 1999.

The reason you should hang on to your records for so long is that the Internal Revenue Service can examine returns as old as seven years. The IRS can't go back any further than that, except in a handful of very special cases. So as long as you keep everything together for at least seven years, you'll almost certainly be okay. (The "handful of very special cases" have to do with businesses with net operating loss carry-forwards and taxpayers with foreign tax credits. If you don't know what these are, they probably don't apply to you anyway. But consult a tax advisor if you're not sure.) If you are ever audited, you can use Money to print a summary of your deductions, and you can verify this report with the canceled checks.

Some documents should be saved for much longer than seven years. When I say to retain records for seven years, I'm referring only to financial records. Hang on to insurance records permanently, for example, because it's possible in some circumstances to file a claim against a policy from years and years ago. Many legal documents should also be retained permanently. (Consult with an attorney for information on this.)

Exporting Reports

Exporting means to move a report to another application. You export reports so that you can manipulate the data in some way or use the data in another document. For example, you might export a report so that you can analyze it in a spreadsheet application such as Microsoft Excel. Or you might want to include a report in a word processing document that you're working on.

TIP

When you export a report, Money creates something called a tab-delimited text file. Tab-delimited text files are easy for spreadsheet applications to import and open, and they can also be imported and opened by most word processing applications.

TIP

To import the tab-delimited text file in another application, just open it from the other application. (You may need to indicate that the exported file uses the .txt extension.)

Export a Report

1 Display the report you want to export.

2 Click the Export button. Money displays the Export Report dialog box.

3 Click the down arrow in the Save In field, and specify where Money should save the exported report.

4 Enter a filename in the File Name text box.

5 Click OK.

6

Personal Financial Planning

Personal financial planning might sound sophisticated, but it's really not. When you boil it down, personal financial planning covers three common-sense activities:

- ◆ Arranging your day-to-day financial affairs so you can spend more time enjoying life rather than worrying about how you're going to pay the bills

- ◆ Picking and then plotting a course toward major, long-term financial goals, such as buying a house, sending the kids to college, or retiring

- ◆ Creating a financial safety net so that a personal tragedy or unexpected expense doesn't mean financial disaster

The Microsoft Money 98 Financial Suite expands the power of the standard version of Money 98 by providing several tips and tools you can use to help you with your financial planning. This section covers these features available only in the Financial Suite. By clicking Planner on the navigation bar, you can access Money's Planner Map, where you can click buttons to use Money's Planning Wizards. You can click Money Insider on the navigation bar to access over 100 personal finance articles written by experts, as well as the Home Inventory worksheet, the How Much Can I Afford worksheet, and the Tax Estimator worksheet.

Describing Yourself

Before you can use any of Money's Planning Wizards, you first need to describe yourself and your finances. Money uses this information along with the accounts and recurring bills you have already created to formulate its financial equations to fit you.

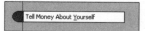

TRY THIS

Take a tour of Money's planning wizards by clicking the Take A Tour button on the Planner Map.

TIP

Right-click an account or an account group and select the shortcut menu's Change Rate command to change the expected rate of return.

Tell Money About Yourself

1. Click Planner on the navigation bar.

2. Click the Tell Money About Yourself button.

3. Enter your name, birthdate, salary, and monthly retirement contribution. Then enter the age at which you plan to retire. Leave the life expectancy set to at least 90, even if this seems a little high.

4. Enter your spouse's name, birthdate, salary, and monthly retirement contribution. Then enter the age at which he or she plans to retire. Once again, leave the life expectancy set to at least 90.

5. Click New and enter the names and birthdates of any dependent children.

6. Click Next to group your accounts by how you use them.

Select an account, and click the Move Account button to move an account to a different group.

Building a Budget

The best way to arrange your day-to-day financial affairs is to summarize how you spend your income and then create guidelines for your spending. Most people call this "budgeting." Once you've decided how you will budget your income and expenses, recording that budget with Money is simple. All you do is describe how much you'll earn or spend in each income or expense category.

TIP

Produce one of Money's Spending Habit reports to use as a guideline in your budgeting. Section 5 describes how you produce reports.

TIP

If you have the standard version of Money 98, you can click Budget on the navigation bar to build a simple budget.

Create a Budget

1 Click Planner on the navigation bar.

2 Click the Make A Budget & Savings Plan button.

3 Click Expenses and Taxes in the Monthly Expenses row to estimate your expenses by month.

4 Click Expense Details to budget by spending category.

5 Select a category from the list box to adjust the budgeted amount for the category.

6 Click an option button to specify whether you want to describe the budgeted amount as a monthly or annual figure.

7 Enter an amount for the spending category.

8 When you're finished, click Close to return to the Budget & Savings Plan window.

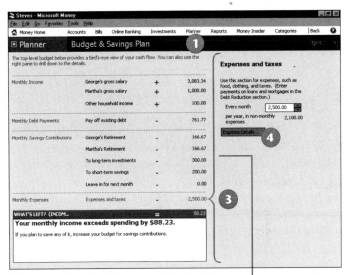

Click a row to adjust the amount in that income or expense category.

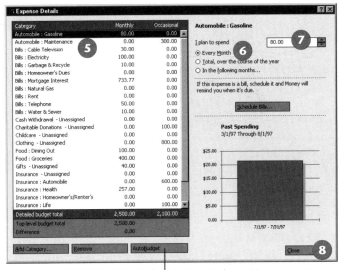

Click the AutoBudget button to have Money create a budget for you based on your previous spending habits.

Six Ways to Stretch Your Budget Dollars

Take Aim at Your Biggest Expenses

If you've been working with Money for any length of time, produce a spending habits report and look at your three largest spending categories. (These spending categories probably constitute most of your spending.) Next, sit down with your family and brainstorm about ways to reduce these expenses.

What you're doing here is only rational. It's much easier to carve out $25 a month of savings in a category in which you're spending $500 a month than it is in a category in which you're spending $50 a month. To save $25 in a $500-a-month expense, you need to figure out how to shave off only 5 percent. To save $25 in a $50-a-month expense, you need to figure out how to chop off 50 percent.

Even if your three biggest spending categories are your housing, car, and grocery bills, if you want to find extra money, you're more likely to succeed by looking wherever you're currently spending the most money. Moving from a 3-bedroom apartment to a 2-bedroom apartment, for example, will save probably 10 percent or more on your housing expenses. So will moving into a smaller house.

If a housing change is too traumatic, consider driving a less expensive, more gas-efficient car or taking the bus. Try to arrange a car pool. If your family uses two cars, consider getting rid of one.

Live Healthier

Here's a strange coincidence. If you make healthy lifestyle choices, you usually save money. Quit smoking, for example, and you easily add $30 or $40 to the monthly cash flow. If you're a heavy smoker, you could add even more. Moderate your alcohol consumption or quit drinking alcohol and you can save just as much money each month. And there are the less obvious healthy choices: drinking less coffee, eating less meat, cutting down on sweets, walking or biking rather than driving.

To find out where you are spending money on bad habits, keep a record of where you spend each and every dollar for a few days. Then look at the list. The following table shows a sample list along with the annual cost of the habit.

ITEM	COST	POSSIBLE YEARLY SAVINGS
Specialty morning coffee	$1.75	$437.50 (if every working day of year)
Cookie after lunch	$0.90	$225.00 (if every working day of year)
Cigarettes	$3.00	$1095.00 (if pack-a-day smoker)
Six-pack after work	$5.00	$520.00 (if two six-packs a week)

Think Green

If you're environmentally conscious, you can also save money. And probably quite a lot. Don't drive if you can walk. Turn your thermostat down a few degrees. Shorten your showers. Turn lights and appliances off when you're not using them. By participating more fully in recycling and composting you can almost eliminate garbage bills. Take good care of your car and make the necessary repairs, and you may be able to drive it for 200,000 miles and keep it out of the junkyard for an extra ten years. If you don't have prejudices about secondhand goods, you can purchase just about anything—clothing, furniture, cars— at great savings. By becoming less of a consumer, you save money and are kind to Mother Earth at the same time.

Stop Using Your Credit Card

In Section 4, I noted that research suggests that people spend about 23 percent more on purchases when they shop with a credit card. If you then pay 15 percent or 20 percent interest on the money you've borrowed with your credit card, you end up paying almost 50 percent more for everything.

Given the propensity to spend more with credit cards, one thing you can probably do to save money is stop using your credit card. If you're skeptical about this gambit, by the way, just try it for a week or two. You may find yourself buying less expensive lunches and not purchasing certain items altogether.

Find One Expense That Wastes Money

Without knowing the specifics of your situation, I suspect you have one or two expenses that, if you didn't make them, would not affect your life at all. For example, do you subscribe to magazines that you never get around to reading? Do you pay to store a boat, RV, antique car, or motorcycle 12 months of the year and only bring it out to enjoy once or twice a year? Consider pulling the plug on the expense. While there probably is some emotional reason for making the expenditure, cutting these kinds of expenses doesn't affect your standard of living.

Find One Expense That You're Willing to Compromise

Another tactic that makes sense is to compromise some area of your spending. Decide right now that you're going to find an area where you will make do with less by living frugally or by making small sacrifices. Then go out and pick the one expenditure in your budget that means the very least to you. Maybe it's athletic club dues. Or the premium cable television stations. This sounds silly, but it usually works. It's often difficult to decide to save, say, $1.00 a day, but it's easier to decide to save a dollar a day by not stopping for coffee on the way to work any more.

6

Calculating Retirement Savings

I may obsess too much about retiring, but I think this is the most important task in this book. I feel this way because so many people aren't preparing for retirement. The irony is that almost everyone can prepare for retirement. If you have a job (it doesn't even have to be a very good job), you can start preparing for retirement.

TIP

For help with retirement planning, click Money Insider on the navigation bar. Then click the Retirement hyperlink from the list on the right.

Calculate How Much You Need to Save for Retirement

1 Click Planner on the navigation bar.

2 Click the Set Lifetime Goals & Events button.

3 Select the retirement goal from the list, click the Edit Goal button, and then select Edit All from the pop-up menu.

4 Click Next until Money displays the dialog box asking for the age at which you plan to retire.

5 See what effect retiring earlier or later would have on your retirement plan by editing the value in this dialog box. Click Next.

6 See what effect working part-time after retirement would have on your retirement plan by editing the value in the top field. Click Next.

7 See what effect a rise or drop in living expenses would have on your retirement plan by clicking a different option button and entering a different value for the expected change in living expenses. Click Next twice.

Average annual returns.
Common stocks have averaged about 10.5 percent over the last 70 years, while long-term bonds have averaged about 5 to 6 percent and small company stocks have averaged 12.5 percent. These are gross return numbers. Your return would be reduced by any investment expenses you pay.

8 Review the figure Money displays for the results of your retirement plan.

9 If applicable, repeat steps 3 through 8 for your spouse.

10 Click the Next button to display a graph of your financial forecast.

11 Optionally, click the Planner bar down arrow, and select Savings & Investments from the menu.

12 Right-click an account, and choose the shortcut menu's Change Rate command to change the expected rate of return for the account.

13 Enter values in the Rate Of Return Before Retirement and Rate Of Return After Retirement fields. Click OK.

14 Click Next to review the financial forecast graph.

6

The First Steps of Retirement Planning

Before you calculate how much you need to save to reach your retirement income goal, you need to set a goal for yourself and also see how much you can save in employer pension plans.

Set a Retirement Income Goal

People throw around all sorts of rules of thumb about this figure. In my case, for example, I figure that I want to live pretty much the same way when I'm retired as I do right now. Of course, when I'm retired, I won't have to make my mortgage payment—my mortgage will have long since been paid by then. And I won't have to pay social security or Medicare taxes—you only pay Social Security and Medicare taxes on earned income, not on unearned income, which is what retirement income is. I also won't have the work expenses, like work clothes and commuting costs, that I now have. So if I take my current income and subtract my mortgage payment, my Social Security and Medicare taxes, and my work expenses, I get a retirement income number that lets me live the same way I do now. Note that if you live in a big house but plan on moving to a small condominium, for example, you can reduce your retirement income goal even more.

The basic calculations you make for determining your retirement income are as follows:

1 Look at your current income.

2 Adjust it for expenses you won't have once you're retired.

The caution I'll give, however, is that you don't want to be too optimistic about reducing your expenses. It's pretty safe to assume that you won't have a mortgage payment when you retire at age 62 if, for example, your mortgage will be paid off by age 59. And while no one knows how the tax laws will change between now and the time you retire, I also think it's pretty safe to assume that your retirement income won't be subject to Social Security and Medicare taxes. But I'd be cautious about assuming you can, for example, tighten up your living expenses. Or get by with just one car if you and your spouse now drive two.

Consider Employer Pension Plans

Before I get into the mechanics of how you go about saving money for retirement, I should say that there is one wildcard here—your employer's pension plan. I think you can probably rely on your employer's pension plan. And it just may be that your employer's pension plan will provide you with all the retirement income you need. But you need to be careful.

One factor that you need to worry about a little is whether your retirement income benefits depend on your continued employment. Let me explain.

One kind of retirement plan, called a *defined benefit plan,* pays you retirement income based on your salary in the final year or years you worked. With this type of plan, for example, you might receive a pension benefit of $32,000 if you work 40 years for a big company and make $40,000 in your final year.

A defined benefit plan such as the one I just described can be a great deal for employees. In fact, if your employer has a plan like this and you can be sure of some day receiving the benefits, you probably don't need to save a dime for retirement. No kidding.

But there's a problem with defined benefit plans if instead of working for one employer for many years, you work for a number of different employers. This is true even if all the employer's have the same "2 percent for every year you work" benefit formula.

The problem is that the figure on which your retirement income is based—your final year's or years' salary—will be very low for all but your last employer or two. Inflation causes this, of course. And so does the fact that people tend to make less in their early working years.

To see how this works, suppose that you work someplace for 40 years, that you're making $40,000 a year in your final years, and that you receive a retirement benefit equal to 2 percent of your final salary for every year you worked. In this case, for your first 10 years of work you would get $8,000 of retirement income (10 x 2% x $40,000). This would be true even though you were probably making far less at that time.

Now consider the case of your neighbor. Let's say she had four different jobs over her working years. Let's say her first job, the one she worked during the first 10 years of her career, paid less because it was a less demanding job. And, of course, 30 years of inflation have passed since she left that job. So maybe her salary at the 10-year marker was $7,000. In this case, for her first 10 years of work she'll get a retirement benefit from that employer of $1,400 (10 x 2% x $40,000).

Do you see the scary part of this? You, for your first 10 years of work, accumulate $8,000 of retirement income, but your neighbor, for her first 10 years of work, accumulates $1,400. Your neighbor's situation is even worse if she switched jobs more frequently—say, every couple of years or so. If that was the case, because of the way that pension benefit calculations work, it's possible for your neighbor to have *no* retirement benefits at all for her first 10 years of work.

What I've just described is, in a nutshell, the problem with defined benefit retirement programs. They can be wonderful deals for long-term employees, but for people who switch jobs frequently, they don't amount to such a good deal. Please note, too, that even if you have the best of intentions about staying someplace for your entire career, you can't really be sure you'll do this. Companies downsize. Industries decline. What you want to do with your life may change.

6

Planning for College

College costs vary widely by region, but generally speaking, four years at a public university cost almost $30,000. Four years at a private university cost around $70,000, and four years at a select private university cost close to $100,000. In spite of the high costs of college, however, your kids can go. As long as you have an idea about what kind of college your child will attend, you can use the Money Financial Suite's Lifetime Goals area to come up with a pretty good guess of how much you need to save.

| Pay college tuition for Margaret (start) |
| Pay college tuition for Margaret (end) |

TIP

For information about college costs, financial aid, student loans, and scholarships, click Money Insider on the navigation bar and then click the College hyperlink from the list on the right.

Determine How Much You Should Save for College

1 Click Planner on the navigation bar.

2 Click the Set Lifetime Goals & Events button.

3 Click the New Goal button.

4 Select Pay Future College Tuition from the list, and click Next.

5 Click the down arrow in the field, and select the name of the person who will attend college. Click Next twice.

6 Enter the age at which this person will enter college, and describe the expected frequency and duration of the tuition bills. Click Next.

7 Enter the current tuition for the college, and estimate the rise in tuition costs.

8 Check the I Plan To Borrow Money To Pay For This box if you plan to take out a college loan. Click Next.

9 If you indicated that you expect to take out a loan to cover college costs, Money displays a dialog box asking you to estimate the costs associated with the loan. Describe the loan, and click Next when you're finished.

10 Estimate how you expect your living expenses to change when the person enters college.

11 Click Next, and then click Finish.

12 To see the effect college tuition has on your financial forecast, click the Planner bar down arrow and select Forecast from the menu.

Investing College Savings

When you start saving money for your child's college expenses, you'll need to decide whose name to put on the savings account. You can hold the savings in your name, in which case you'll be taxed on the investment income the savings produce, or you can give the savings to your child, in which case your child will be taxed. In general, you pay less income tax by putting money in your child's name. If the child is 14 years old or less, the first $600 or so of investment income is tax-free and the next $600 is taxed at the lowest marginal income tax rate. If the child is 15 years old or more, the first $3,400 of income is tax-free (this might include both investment income and earned income if the child now has a job) and roughly the next $20,000 of income is taxed at the lowest marginal rate.

The one awkward thing about putting the money in a child's name is that the money really does become the child's. You can't borrow it temporarily—even if you have a good reason to. And when children reach the age of majority, either 18 or 21, they can spend the money on anything they want.

The other tricky thing about deciding whether to put the savings in the child's or in the parent's name has to do with current financial aid regulations. These regulations assume that basically all of a child's savings are available for college but only a portion of his or her parent's savings are available.

In spite of the risks, I recommend using a custodial account to save money for college expenses if you're going to initiate a long-term, substantial college savings program. If you're not going to initiate a long-term, substantial savings program, I'd say go ahead and keep the money in your name.

Where Should You Invest College Savings Money?

As long as you start early—preferably while your child is still in diapers and definitely not long after your child starts grade school—I think it makes sense to invest college savings money in the stock market. Go for something that's well-diversified and inexpensive. (A no-load stock index fund based on the Standard & Poors 500 is what I've got my kids' college money in.)

If you figure on the stock market delivering its historical average of 10 percent and you subtract about .2 percent for expenses, you can figure on your college savings money earning about 9.8 percent. That's pretty good.

Then, at some point in the future, you'll want to begin moving money from the stock market into something very safe. Some financial writers advocate moving money from stocks to short-term bonds or certificates of deposit four to five years before you need it. This means moving a child's college freshman year money from the stock market to bonds at roughly the time the child is a high school freshman. Move more money into safer investments in each of the next three years to provide for the child's sophomore, junior, and senior years of college.

Editing College Savings Goals

Once you have created a goal for paying future college tuition, you can easily edit this goal if you find that it isn't within your financial reach or if your college plans change.

TIP

About financial aid and scholarships. *Unless you've already been through the college financial aid process, you probably think there is more "free money" than there really is. In any case, it's well worth the trouble of filling out the Free Application for Federal Student Aid to see if your child qualifies for a federal grant, low-interest loan, or work-study program. You can pick up this form at your local library. You should also encourage your child to apply for all private scholarships he or she qualifies for.*

Edit Your College Savings Goal

1. Click Planner on the navigation bar.

2. Click the Set Lifetime Goals & Events button.

3. Select the Pay College Tuition goal from the list, and click the Edit Goal button.

4. Select Edit All from the pop-up menu.

5. Go through the dialog boxes again to see what effects choosing a different college or taking out a college loan would have on your financial forecast.

6. Review the financial forecast information in the last dialog box, and click Finish.

7. To see what effect the new college tuition goal has on your financial forecast, click the Planner bar down arrow and select Forecast from the menu.

What to Do If You Can't Afford College

Even if you can't afford a dime for your kid's college education, your kids can still figure out a way to go to college and even on to graduate and professional school. They will have to be a bit more flexible. They may need to be a bit more creative. But with some work and planning—and perhaps, more importantly, the desire—any kid can go to college. It's more important to offer emotional support and encouragement than cold, hard cash.

I should also mention that the calculation method I described earlier in this section probably overstates the amount you need to save for college. The calculations I described assume that you need to have all the money saved by the time your child starts college. (Remember, however, that you won't need to pay the sophomore, junior, and senior year expenses until the following years.) For this reason, don't worry if you can only save, say, 50 or 75 percent of what your calculations show as necessary. If you can just start saving money regularly—especially if you start early—you can make wonderful progress in your saving.

Let me also mention that I have several friends who successfully and solely paid their ways through both college and graduate and professional school. They all describe the experience as positive and a source of real pride. But enough said. Let's look at the down-and-dirty mechanics of saving serious money.

Basically, saving for college comes down to reducing either of the variables in the following formula:

Annual College Costs x Years of College = Total College Costs

If you start brainstorming, you can quickly come up with a lot of good ideas for reducing the costs of college. In the lists that follow, I describe the best ways I know of to reduce annual college costs as well as the number of years it takes to complete college.

Here are ways to reduce the cost of going to college:

◆ Attend a community college for the first two years rather than a public university. This saves $8,000 over the first two years.

◆ Attend an equivalent public university instead of a private university. This saves $28,000 over four years

◆ Live at home rather than in student housing and attend a college as a commuter student. Your savings with this tactic are about $1,200 a year (the net of commuting costs).

◆ Get a part-time student job, such as a dormitory resident assistant. This saves $3,000 (usually paid as free room and board).

◆ Do a one-quarter work-for-credit study that pays a real salary. This saves $3,000 in earnings during the quarter.

◆ Work at the college as a full-time employee. Many colleges will then allow you to take a part-time class load for free or for a nominal fee.

Here are ways to reduce the amount of time spent in college:

◆ Take Advanced Placement (AP) classes in high school. (If your child's high school doesn't offer advanced placement classes, you can also arrange for College Level Examination Program, or CLEP, examinations.) Many high schools offer half a dozen AP classes and some offer twice that many.

◆ Take a transferable community college class during the summer breaks. You can shave off one quarter or even a semester this way.

◆ Take an extra class a year. Or take an extra class each quarter or semester if you can take the extra class for free.

I know that some of the tricks and techniques included in the two preceding lists aren't exactly appealing. But if someone has to choose between going to college on a shoe-string budget or not going at all, college on a shoe-string budget is the better choice, by far.

Applying for Financial Aid

To determine whether a student is eligible for financial aid, you fill out the Free Application for Federal Student Aid, or FAFSA. The information you provide on this statement determines the amount the government and colleges expect you to contribute to your child's educational expenses. The financial aid formulas expect you to live at the poverty line—around $15,000 for a family of four—and then contribute between 10 and 20 percent of the income you make in excess of the poverty line to your child's college expenses. Your child is expected to earn and contribute about $1,000 per year and pay whatever savings he or she has toward the expense of college. Whatever amount is left over after deducting these amounts determines the amount of financial aid the student is eligible for.

Financial aid comes in three types: grants, loans, and work study programs. Grants are "free money" that doesn't need to be repaid, but are available to only the neediest of students. College loans are much more prevalent, and loans are available in several forms. Some loans are given to parents, while others are given to students. Some loans are through a bank while other times the federal government loans you the money directly. Some loans are need-based and do not require you to pay interest on the loan until the student graduates from college, while other loans are unsubsidized and not based on need. Lastly, work study programs allow qualified students to help pay for their college costs by working for an approved employer, often on campus. To find out more about financial aid programs available at the college your child plans on attending, inquire at the college's financial aid office.

6

Saving for Major Purchases or Events

The savings goals discussed earlier in this section all assume that you will slowly withdraw the money you saved over a period of years. Other savings goals use calculations that assume you will take the saved money out in one large lump sum. These types of goals are useful for planning for the purchase of a new car; for saving for a wedding, bar mitzvah, or other important celebration; or saving for a down payment on a house.

TIP

Over the last 70 years, annual inflation has averaged 3.1 percent.

Save for a Large Purchase

1 Click Planner on the navigation bar.

2 Click the Set Lifetime Goals & Events button.

3 Click the New Goal button.

4 Select either Buy a Car, Pay for a Large Future Expense, Pay for a Wedding, or Pay for a Vacation from the list box, depending on your goal. Click Next.

5 Name the goal and click Next.

6 Describe when the purchase or event should take place and click Next.

TIP

Money doesn't let you change the expected rise of wedding or vacation costs. If you expect these costs to rise between now and the time the wedding or vacation takes place, use the Pay For A Large Future Expense goal to describe these events.

TIP

To delete a goal, select it from the Lifetime Goals list and click the Delete Goal button.

7 Enter the cost of the purchase or event in today's dollars.

8 Describe the rate at which you expect the costs to rise between now and the time the purchase will occur.

9 If you plan on taking out a loan for the purchase, check the I Plan To Borrow Money To Pay For This box. Click Next.

10 If you indicated that you would take out a loan for the purchase, Money asks you a few questions about the loan. Fill out the dialog box, and then click Next.

11 Click Finish. To see what effect the goal has on your financial forecast, click the Planner bar down arrow and choose Forecast from the menu.

6

Tracking Income and Tax Deductions

If you itemize your deductions or have business expenses, using Money for your record-keeping can save you hundreds of dollars a year in taxes because you can keep an exhaustive list of your deductions.

To use Money for tax-deduction record-keeping, all you need to do is use categories that mesh nicely with the tax deductions you intend to take. Money supplies a Categories list that you can modify as need be. Once you have a Categories list built to suit your needs, just categorize all of your transactions during the year. At the end of the year you can then create a Tax-Related Transactions report, which you can use to fill out your tax returns.

SEE ALSO

For information on creating a Tax-Related Transactions report, see page 55.

Add a Tax-Deduction Category to Your Categories List

1 Click Categories on the navigation bar.

2 Click the New button.

3 Click the Create A New Category option button, and click Next.

4 Enter a name for the new tax-deduction category in the Name field.

5 Specify whether the new category is an income or an expense category by clicking the appropriate option button, and click Next.

6 Select a category group that best describes the new category from the list box.

7 Click Finish to add the new category to the categories list.

8 Select the new category from the list, and click the Go To Category button.

TRY THIS

Using the Tax Estimator.
Use the Money 98 Financial Suite Tax Estimator to estimate your taxes for the coming year. Click Money Insider on the navigation bar. Click the Tax Worksheet hyperlink from the list on the right. Use the Overview, Income, Deductions, and Adjustments tabs to describe your filing status, estimated income, and deductions. Click the Analysis tab to see approximately how much you will owe in taxes and whether or not you're withholding enough.

9 Check the Include On Tax Reports box.

10 Click the down arrow in the Tax Form field, and select the tax form to which the new category applies.

11 Click the down arrow in the Form Line field, and select the appropriate line from that tax form.

12 Click the Categories & Payees button to return to the Categories List window, and repeat steps 3 through 13 to add the income and expense categories you need.

The Five Best Ways to Save Money on Taxes

Take Every Deduction You're Entitled To

I continually run into people who don't take all the deductions they're entitled to. Some of them think they increase their risk of being audited by taking too many deductions. Others think maybe they're being a little unpatriotic by taking too many deductions. But not taking every deduction you're entitled to is a big mistake. The U.S. Congress writes the tax laws with the assumption that taxpayers will take every deduction to which they're entitled.

If you routinely give away clothing your kids have outgrown to the local thrift shop, for example, be sure to collect a receipt, assign a fair value, and then take the amount as a charitable donation deduction. If you're spending money on night school so that you can acquire new skills and get better job, take the amount as an employee business expense deduction.

Bunch Your Deductions

Perhaps the best way to save money on income taxes without giving up anything in return is to bunch your deductions so you take the standard deduction in some years and itemize deductions in other years. This effectively increases your deductions. Let me explain. Let's say you're married and that you routinely have about $8,000 a year in itemized deductions.

Furthermore, just to make the math simple, let's also assume that you can take a $7,000 standard deduction. In any given year, then, it makes sense to take the $8,000 a year in itemized deductions because that reduces your income tax bill. But if you pay some deductions early and some deductions late, you can actually increase the total deductions you're taking over time. Why? Because (and this is the trick) in the years when your itemized deductions fall below the standard deduction amount, you can take the standard deduction. Let me show you how this works over a four-year time frame.

Let's say that your plan is to use the standard $7,000 deduction in years 1 and 3 and itemized deductions in years 2 and 4. In this case, you want to pay as many of your deductions as you can in years 2 and 4. The table below shows an example of what your itemized deductions could be in years 1, 2, 3, and 4 if you did this kind of juggling.

ITEMIZED DEDUCTION	YEAR 1	YEAR 2	YEAR 3	YEAR 4
Mortgage interest	$5,500	$6,500	$5,000	$7,000
Real estate taxes	0	$3,000	0	$3,000
Charitable donations	0	$2,000	0	$2,000
Total	$5,500	$11,500	$5,000	$12,000

Because you get to choose whether to itemize or use the standard deduction, you itemize in years 2 and 4, but you take the standard deduction in years 1 and 3. If you itemize in each of the four years, you'll have $32,000 of deductions (four years times $8,000 a year). If you simply take the standard deduction, you'll have $28,000 of deductions (four years times $7,000). But by bunching your deductions and then flip-flopping between the standard deduction and itemized deductions, you can deduct $37,500.

Exploit Retirement Savings Options

Tax-deferred investment options like 401(k)s, 403(b)s, IRAs, SEP/IRAs, and Keoghs are such good deals that I can't promote them enough. If you're saving for retirement (and you should be), these tax-deferred investment options are absolutely the best way to go.

Don't Use Nondeductible Consumer Credit

Another very powerful tax-savings gambit is to convert nondeductible consumer credit interest on items such as car loans, credit cards, personal lines of credit, and so forth to deductible mortgage or home equity loan interest. To do this, you need to be a homeowner, of course. But assuming you are, you could take out, say, a $25,000 second mortgage home equity loan and use the proceeds to pay off your car loan, all your credit cards, a student loan you're still paying on, and any other debts you have.

If you swap $25,000 of consumer credit that charges 10 percent interest with a $25,000 home equity loan that charges 10 percent, for example, you still pay $2,500 a year of interest, but you can use the $2,500 of home equity loan interest as a deduction. If your marginal, or highest, income tax rate is 28 percent, you save about $700 a year. If the home equity loan's interest rate happens to be lower than the average interest rate you're paying on all the consumer credit you replace—and it probably is—you save even more money.

Despite the substantial savings available, I caution you regarding this particular gambit, especially if you're someone who likes to use a credit card. Sure, if you do one of these home equity loan things and use the proceeds to pay off your consumer credit debt, it may save on taxes. But you won't be in any better shape if you go out and start charging up your credit cards again. More than a few people take aout a home equity loan and then find themselves with both a $25,000 home equity loan and a bunch of new credit card debts.

Let me mention one other problem: you could end up stretching out the repayment of your debt. Swapping a deductible home equity loan for a nondeductible car loan sounds like a good idea. And it really may save on taxes. But you might not get ahead if your car loan has 3 years of payments left and your new home equity loan lets you make payments over the next 10 years.

6

Tracking Assets and Liabilities

Microsoft Money's strength lies in keeping records of financial assets like bank accounts, money-market funds, and investments, as well as in tracking liabilities such as mortgages and credit cards. But besides tracking these sorts of assets and liabilities, you can also use Money to track whatever else you own. By doing so, you can produce net worth reports. If you're a homeowner, you can even keep a record of the improvements you've made to your home—and that can save on taxes later on.

Microsoft Money 98 Financial Suite also comes with powerful tools for analyzing loans and for monitoring the money you borrow. Using these tools as part of your regular financial record-keeping can deliver enormous benefits. By monitoring the money you borrow and what that money costs you (in interest), you can do a much better job of planning and managing your day-to-day financial affairs. You'll also be able to calculate your net worth more accurately. By using Money to carefully analyze the loans you consider, you can easily save thousands of dollars in interest and finance charges.

Creating Asset Accounts

To track your net worth, you set up asset accounts for each major asset you own: your house, the car or cars you drive, and any other large, valuable items. You may also want to set up a catchall account for tracking the items that perhaps aren't especially valuable individually but collectively add up to a significant value, things like baseball cards or silverware.

House

TIP

If you're setting up an asset account for a house, enter the house's original cost.

Create an Asset Account

1. Click Accounts on the navigation bar once or twice to display the Account Manager window.

2. Click the New Account button.

3. The wizard asks for the name of the bank or institution where the Account is held. Leave the field empty, and click Next.

4. Select Asset from the list, and click Next.

5. Enter a name for the asset account, and click Next.

6. Enter the current value of the asset or its original cost.

7. Specify whether or not a loan account is associated with the asset account, and click Next.

8. If a loan account is associated with the asset account, click the down arrow in the field and select the loan account from the list.

9. Click Finish.

Tracking Assets

Once you've set up an asset account, it isn't difficult to keep a record of the asset and track the changes in its value. As with recording a check in a bank account register, you use the transaction forms at the bottom of the Account Register window to track changes to the value of an asset.

TRY THIS

If you're recording an increase in value, Money objects if you attempt to use an expense category to categorize the transaction. To avoid this problem, you can create a category to describe depreciation and appreciation of assets by entering "Market Adjustment" in the Category field.

Track an Asset

1. Display the register for the asset account.

2. Click the Decrease or Increase tab, depending on whether you're describing a negative or positive change in the asset's value.

3. Enter the date of the change.

4. Optionally, enter the name of the person or business you paid if you made improvements on the asset.

5. Enter the amount of the change.

6. Click the down arrow in the Category field, and select a spending category.

7. Optionally, enter a description of the change.

8. Click Enter to record the increase or decrease and recalculate the asset account's balance.

Tips for Tracking Assets

Asset accounts work very much like bank accounts, and the mechanics of keeping track of an asset with Money are straightforward. Asset record-keeping, however, can be a little tricky.

Your Home

A home is usually a person's single largest asset. If you own a home and have decided to track your net worth with Money, you'll want to set up a home, or personal residence, account and use it to track the value of your home.

The historical appreciation of real estate makes it tempting to track the fair market value of a home. However, it makes more sense to track the original cost of the home as well as the cost of any home improvements. The reason for this is that in general, the gains you realize when you sell a house are taxed as income. There are, however, two instances when the capital gains on the sale of a house are not taxed as income. You don't have to pay income tax on a gain if you purchase another home of equal or greater value within 24 months of selling the home. Also, taxpayers age 55 or older are allowed to ignore, once, up to $125,000 of gain on the sale of a primary residence.

Even if you think that one of the two capital gains exceptions might apply to you, it makes sense to keep a record of your home's cost as well as the cost of improvements you make to it. There's no harm in doing so, the work is extremely minimal, and you might someday save a lot of money (because the two exceptions mentioned earlier might not apply).

To keep a record of a home's cost and the cost of improvements, you first set up an asset account named something like "Home" or "Residence." (I described how to do this on page 89.) In this account, you record as transactions the original cost of the home as well as associated purchase costs such as escrow fees and title insurance. In the future, whenever you spend money to improve your home, you transfer the money from your checking account to the asset account set up for your home.

What qualifies as an improvement? Anything that adds value to a home or to its useful life. For example, adding a swimming pool, finishing the basement, and landscaping the site all qualify as improvements. However, maintenance costs such as those for painting the exterior or interior, repairing a leaky roof, or fixing faulty electrical wiring don't qualify as improvements.

The only problem to this approach is that your financial records don't show the value of your home—only the total of its cost and any improvements. If you

want to also show the home's value, you can add a transaction to your asset register that adjusts the account's total to the home's market value. Just be sure to delete this transaction before you calculate the capital gain stemming from the sale of the home

Cars, Boats, and Other Personal Property

Cars, boats, and other valuable personal property can usually be handled nicely with individual accounts. In general, you don't need to make a lot of adjustments to the value of these assets. And you probably won't make improvements that increase their value, anyway. So you may just want to periodically—say, at the end of each year—update the account balances so that the asset's ending balance approximates its fair market value.

Asset Lists for Property and Casualty Insurance

It's not a bad idea to maintain records of the assets you've insured with a property insurance policy. The reason for this is probably clear: if disaster strikes, a list of the insured items can make claim reports and collections easier and more complete.

If you have Money 98 Financial Suite, you can create this list using the Home Inventory Worksheet. To access the Home Inventory Worksheet, click Money Insider on the navigation bar and then click the Home Inventory Worksheet hyperlink from the list on the right. Add possessions to your property list by clicking the appropriate category tab on the left and then clicking the New button. If you don't have Money 98 Financial Suite, you can set up another asset account called something like "Personal Property" and carefully list all assets you've insured. The more information on your list, the better. If possible, include information such as model numbers and original costs. Remember that you can use the Split Transaction dialog box to store additional data. Another great way to create an asset list for insured personal property (such as the contents of your home) is to walk through your house with a video camera and record what's in each room. You can also provide narrative descriptions of the items you're filming as you shoot the video.

One other point. Your asset list won't do much good if your computer and all your backup disks or your video tape are lost in a fire or flood (or whatever casualty destroys or damages the property you've insured). For this reason, you should probably keep an up-to-date copy of your asset list in a secure place such as a safe-deposit box.

Setting Up Loan Accounts

Tracking a loan with Money is very easy, especially if you're already familiar and comfortable with tracking a bank account and you know how to transfer money between accounts. To begin tracking a loan, all you need to do is find the paperwork that describes the loan and its current balance (probably the last monthly statement) and then use the New Account Wizard to set up an account for the loan.

Mortgage

TIP

If you're describing an adjustable rate mortgage, enter the date of the next adjustment and the length of the period between adjustments.

TIP

If you have made previous payments, Money asks how far back it should go to calculate the loan payments and amortization.

Create a Loan Account

1. Click Accounts on the navigation bar once or twice to display the Account Manager window.

2. Click the New Account button.

3. Enter the name of the bank or financial institution to whom you'll make your payments, and click Next.

4. Select Loan from the list, and click Next three times.

5. Click the Borrowing Money option button, and click Next.

6. Enter the loan name and the lender, and click Next.

7. Specify whether the loan is a fixed or adjustable rate mortgage, and click Next.

8. Specify whether or not you have already made payments on the loan, and click Next.

9. Enter the date when you made the first loan payment, and click Next twice.

10. Select a payment frequency from the drop-down list box, and click Next.

11. Select the option that corresponds to your interest calculation method, and click Next.

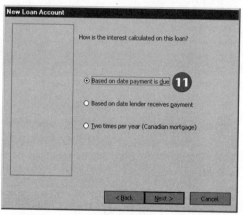

12 Enter four of the five loan calculation variables—the loan balance, the interest rate, the scheduled loan length, the combined principal and interest payment, and the balloon payment—in the dialog boxes Money provides. Click Next.

13 Click OK to accept the loan variable Money calculated for you, and review the summary Money provides. Click Next twice to continue.

14 Specify whether the loan is a house loan, and click Next.

15 Specify whether the loan is tax-deductible, and click Next.

16 Enter the date you want to be reminded of the loan payment and the bank account from which you'll make the payment, and click Next.

17 Specify whether or not an asset account is associated with the loan. If so, select the asset account from the list box. Click Finish.

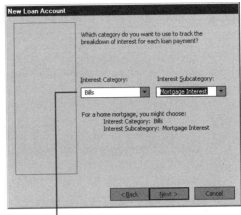

Select the principal and interest categories and subcategories, and click Next.

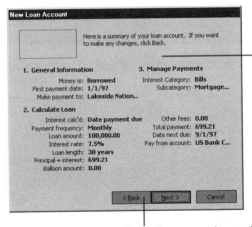

After you've entered all of the loan account information, Money summarizes the loan.

If you discover you've made a mistake, click Back to backtrack your way through the New Loan Account Wizard's dialog boxes.

Setting Up Liability Accounts

If your loan won't be amortized, you set up a liability account instead of a loan account. Setting up a liability account works very much like setting up other accounts.

Eastern City
Bank Liability

Create a Liability Account

1. Click Accounts on the navigation bar once or twice to display the Account Manager window.

2. Click the New Account button.

3. Enter the name of the bank or financial institution to whom you'll make your payments, and click Next.

4. Select Liability from the list, and click Next.

5. Enter a name for the liability account, and click Next.

6. Enter the ending liability balance (the amount you still owe) from your last statement, and click Next.

7. Click the I Have No Other Accounts At This Bank option button, and click Next.

8. Click the No, Not Now option button, and click Finish.

Entering Liability Account Payments

If you set up a liability account, you record in your checking account any check that pays interest or principal for the liability in the usual way.

Record a Liability Account Payment

1. Display the register for the checking account from which you want to write the liability account payment.

2. Click the Check tab (or the Withdrawal tab if the loan payment is automatically withdrawn from your account), and if necessary, click New.

3. Enter the check number.

4. Enter the check date.

5. Enter the lender's name.

6. Enter the payment.

7. Describe the payment in the Category fields, or click the Split button to record a check that pays both interest and principal.

8. If you're splitting the transaction, use the Split Transaction dialog box to categorize each part of the transaction.

9. Click Enter to record the payment.

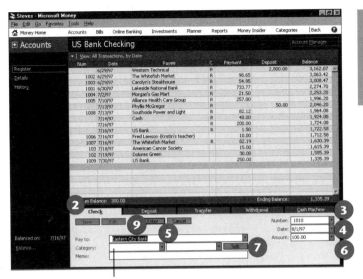

If you record a check that pays only interest, categorize it as an interest expense.

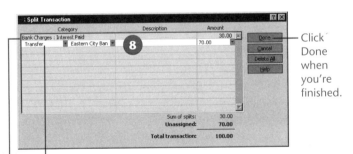

Click Done when you're finished.

Describe the principal part of the payment on the second line by recording a transfer to the liability account.

Describe the interest part of the payment on the first line, and categorize it as an interest expense.

Fixing Loan Account Balance Errors

Even though Money calculates the interest and principal portions of the loan payments you make, Money's calculations might still be wrong. This is especially true if the interest calculation is based on the date the payment is received by the lender. In this case, a delay in the mail of just a few days can create a difference in Money's calculation of the interest and the lender's calculation of the interest. Fortunately, it's easy to fix these kinds of errors.

Balanced On: 8/1/97

TIP

It's a good idea to balance your loan account each time you get a monthly statement.

Correct a Loan Account Balance

1. Display the register for the loan account.

2. Click Balance Account on the Accounts bar.

3. Enter the ending balance from your monthly statement.

4. Enter the ending date from your monthly statement.

5. If any fees are not accounted for in your records, categorize the fees in the Category fields.

6. Click OK to adjust the balance.

Using the Home Worksheet

Money 98 Financial Suite includes a Home Worksheet that lets you calculate how much of a loan payment you can afford. Often, calculating a loan payment is the first step you make when you assess a loan. Before you even consider buying a new car or house, for example, you want to make sure that you can afford to make the payments.

TIP

Click the Set A Goal button to add a Purchase A Home goal to your Lifetime Goals list.

Calculate a Loan Payment

1. Click Money Insider on the navigation bar.

2. Click the Home Worksheet hyperlink from the list on the right.

3. Click the Information tab.

4. Enter your gross monthly income, any debt you are currently paying off, and the percent down the mortgage requires.

5. Click the Loan Details tab.

6. Enter the loan's length and the interest rate.

7. Enter any points, mortgage insurance costs, property taxes, and closing costs associated with the loan.

8. Adjust the debt and income ratios if necessary.

9. Click the Set A Goal tab to review the total costs associated with the mortgage and to see what price range you should be looking at.

When to Repay and Refinance Mortgages

To determine whether it makes sense to repay a mortgage (or any other debt) early, you need to compare the interest rate the loan charges with the interest rate or investment return that some other investment pays. The rule is simple: your loan's interest rate needs to exceed the investment's interest rate or investment return in order for early loan repayment to make sense. If your mortgage charges 8 percent interest but you can buy a bond that pays 10 percent, for example, you shouldn't "invest" your money by repaying your mortgage early. You end up with more money by investing in the 10 percent bonds.

As a general rule, too, I should tell you that except in unusual situations (when your mortgage interest rate is in double-digits, for example), early mortgage repayment is probably not all that great a deal. If you can stick more money in your employer's 401(k) or 403(b) plan or in a tax-deductible individual retirement account (IRA), the 401(k), 403(b), or IRA always beats early mortgage repayment. In fact, it's not even a contest.

What About Your Other Debt?

While you get truly awesome interest savings when you look at the effect of repaying a long-term loan like a mortgage early, it's really a better deal to get out from under your credit card debt and other consumer credit debt.

Interest on consumer credit such as credit cards and car loans isn't tax-deductible. So a credit card that charges, say, 16 percent, really does cost 16 percent, whereas an 8 percent mortgage doesn't really cost 8 percent. Depending on your income tax situation, you get a tax deduction that effectively lowers your 8 percent mortgage to something between 5 percent and 7 percent. In effect, by paying off a credit card that charges a 16 percent interest rate, you make a 16 percent profit on your investment. (Your investment is paying off the credit card early.) If you pay off a mortgage that charges an effective, after-income-taxes-are-figured, interest rate of 5 percent, you make a 5 percent profit on your investment.

There's one other point that I should make about early repayment of debts. The idea is sound, but it doesn't really pay off if you go out and replace your old debt with new debt. Okay, that sounds funny. But let me explain. Paying off your mortgage early sounds like a great deal—and it is a great deal, really. But if you pay your mortgage off early and then, because you don't have mortgage payments, go out and purchase a new, larger, more expensive home, you're not really getting ahead. And if you get that credit card paid off early, but then you go out and fill your closet with a dazzling new wardrobe, you're not getting ahead that way either.

If you're paying a mortgage, it's easy to wonder whether you should refinance when interest rates drop. The logic seems straightforward enough: replace an expensive mortgage with a cheap mortgage and save money. Unfortunately, figuring out whether you'll actually save by refinancing a mortgage is very difficult.

Refinancing in a Nutshell

The trick to refinancing a mortgage is to make sure that you pay less for the new mortgage—taking into account both the interest charges and any refinancing costs—than you pay for your existing mortgage. To see if you pay less, you need to consider the interest rate and the refinancing costs, of course, but you also need to think about how long you'll be paying interest.

Fortunately, you can use the Mortgage Planner to perform this analysis. You use the Mortgage Planner as described in the preceding section, but with several minor twists.

When you describe your existing mortgage as the first mortgage (Mortgage A), don't worry about the loan fees and payments you've already made. For your existing

mortgage, then, there aren't discount points, loan service fees, or closing costs. And for your existing mortgage, the loan balance and the scheduled loan length equal what is left for you to pay, not what you originally had to pay.

Does all that make sense? Think about it for a minute and it should. When you consider refinancing a loan, you basically compare two loans: your existing loan, for which you'll pay no extra discount points, no loan service fees, and no closing costs, and a new mortgage, for which you'll pay all these extra charges.

The Complicating Factor

Unfortunately, there's also a complicating factor when it comes to mortgage refinancing. If you want to refinance as a way to save money over the long haul, you shouldn't do it as a way to stretch out your payments. In other words, you're very unlikely to save money by replacing an existing mortgage that has 15 years of payments left with a new, refinanced mortgage that requires 30 years of payments. Even if the new mortgage's interest rate is much lower, you'll be borrowing the money for a lot longer with the new mortgage.

Using the Loan Worksheet

You can save yourself money—sometimes lots and lots of money—by carefully considering all your options when you shop for a new mortgage. Thankfully, Money 98 Financial Suite provides a very powerful, very sophisticated worksheet with which you can compare two mortgages and determine whether or not it makes sense to refinance a mortgage.

TIP

Be careful not to count the same fee twice. For example, don't enter a loan fee once in the Points field and then again in the Loan Service Fee field.

TIP

Click the Variable Rate tab and use its boxes to describe adjustable rate mortgages.

Compare Two Mortgages

1 Click Money Insider on the navigation bar.

2 Click the Loan Worksheet hyperlink from the list on the right.

3 Click the Initial Costs tab.

4 Describe the down payments required by both mortgages.

5 Specify any closing costs you'll pay.

6 Specify the discount points you'll pay to secure the loan.

7 Specify any loan service fee you'll pay.

8 Click the Loan Terms tab and specify the length of the loan.

9 Specify the interest rate

10 Specify the balloon payment amount, if there is one.

11 Click the Comparison tab.

12 Enter how long you expect to hold the loan.

13 Review the break-even point Money calculates for the mortgages.

8

Investing in Stocks, Bonds, and Mutual Funds

Microsoft Money provides wonderful tools for investment record-keeping. If you're an investor, you've probably already considered whether and how to use Money to make investment record-keeping easier and less time-consuming.

In general, there are two good reasons for using Money to track your investments.

◆ Your investments affect your income taxes. If you have investments that aren't tax deferred, you need to track your investments with Money so that you know the taxable investment income that your investments produce and so you know about any capital gains or losses that occur (which will be taxable) when you sell an investment.

◆ You want to use Money's investment reports to assess the performance of your investments because you can't get annual investment return information somewhere else. By using Money's investment performance report, you can calculate the rate of return for the investments you're holding.

To get started with investment record-keeping, set up investment accounts and describe your current investment portfolio. After you complete these preliminary tasks, you can use Money for day-to-day financial record-keeping.

Setting Up Investment Accounts

To track your investments, set up at least one investment account. The general rule is to set up one investment account for each brokerage account statement you receive.

Vanguard
Investment

TIP

If you're investing money in tax-deferred accounts (and this is a smart thing to do), you won't have any taxable investment income because you won't have any capital gains or losses from your investments, so you don't really need to use Money to track this account.

Set Up an Investment Account

1 Click Accounts on the navigation bar once or twice to display the Account Manager window.

2 Click the New Account button.

3 Optionally, enter the name of the financial institution associated with the account, and click Next.

4 Select Investment from the list of accounts, and click Next.

5 Enter a name for the investment account, and click Next.

6 Specify whether or not the account is tax deferred, and click Next.

7 Enter the estimated value of the investments in the account.

8 Specify whether or not the account has an associated cash account, and click Next.

If you're setting up one investment account for each monthly statement, you may want to provide the name of the mutual-fund management company or stock brokerage company.

If you're investing exclusively in mutual funds, certificates of deposit (CDs), money-market accounts, or U.S. savings bonds you don't need Money's investment accounts to monitor the performance of your investments. You can simply record the dividend or interest income you earn when you deposit it into your checking account. You can also tell how well these investments are doing by looking at their interest rates or annual returns.

Most brokerage accounts have an associated cash account, which is just a checking or money market account that you use to either collect the cash you receive from investments or to provide cash for investments.

9 If the investment has an associated cash account, enter the cash account's ending balance from your last monthly statement and click Next.

10 Select the option that best corresponds with the way you use the investment account, and click Next twice.

11 If you entered a financial institution name in step 3, click the I Have No Other Accounts At This Bank option button and click Next.

12 When Money asks if you want to set up the account for online banking, click the No, Not Now option button and click Finish.

8

Describing Your Portfolio

Once you've set up your investment account, you're ready to describe the investments in your portfolio. You need to create these individual investments so that you can work with them later.

TIP

It's usually a good idea to enter each investment lot separately if you purchased different lots at different prices. If you don't want to go to this much work, however, you can just enter all of the lots together as one big lot and use the average price you paid.

Describe Your Current Portfolio

1. Display the investment account's register.

2. Click New.

3. Enter the date you first purchased the investment.

4. Enter a name for the investment.

5. Click Enter to display the Create New Investment dialog box.

6. Select the option that most closely describes the investment you're adding, and click Next.

7. Use the fields that Money provides to describe the investment in more detail, and click Finish.

8. Click the down arrow in the Activity field, and select Buy from the list.

9. Enter the number of shares you own.

10. Enter the cost per unit you paid.

11. Enter any sales commission you paid.

12. Review the contents of the Total field, and edit them if necessary.

13. Delete the account name shown in the Transfer From field. You don't want to reduce the cash balance for this transaction if it's an old investment purchase.

14. Click Enter to record the investment.

If you plan to use Money's Online Quotes feature, enter the security symbol.

8

Updating Prices

After you've described all the investments in your portfolio, you're ready to enter current price information. You'll want to do this so your investment records reflect current market values.

Update the Prices in Your Portfolio

1 Display the investment account register.

2 Click Update Price on the Accounts bar.

3 Click the down arrow in the Investment field, and select the investment whose current market price you want to update.

4 Enter the current date.

5 Enter the current market price.

6 Click Update.

7 Repeat steps 3 through 6 for the other investments you're holding.

8 Click Close.

The Investment
Portfolio Window

Once you've set up your investment accounts, described your investments, and updated their prices, you can use the Investment Portfolio window to monitor your investments. To display the Investment Portfolio window, click Investments on the navigation bar.

This view shows gain and return figures for your investments

This view displays the latest quotes for your investments.

This view charts the distribution of funds by investment type.

This window lists your investments.

Click one of the tabs to view your investments in a different way.

Select an investment, and then click the Go To button to display the account details for that investment.

Recording Investment Purchases

After you've set up your investment accounts and described your current portfolio, you're ready to begin using Money for day-to-day record-keeping. Whenever you purchase more shares of a stock or mutual fund or additional bonds, you describe the purchase in the investment account's Account Register window.

TIP

If you haven't purchased the stock, bond, or mutual fund before, when you enter the name in the Investment field, Money displays the Create New Investment dialog box where you can set up the investment.

TIP

To describe a purchase or sale, you need to enter at least three of the following four inputs: Quantity, Price, Commission, and Total. If you leave one of these inputs blank, Money uses the other three inputs to calculate the fourth.

Record a Purchase

1. Display the investment account register.

2. Click New.

3. Enter the purchase date.

4. Enter a name for the investment, or select it from the list.

5. Click the down arrow in the Activity field, and select Buy from the list.

6. Indicate the number of stock or mutual fund shares or the number of individual bonds you're purchasing.

7. Enter the dollar price per share or the price per bond.

8. Record any sales commission you paid.

9. Verify the contents of the Total field, and edit them, if necessary, to correctly reflect the total purchase price.

10. Click the down arrow in the Transfer From field, and select the bank account or associated cash account you are using to pay for the purchase.

11. Click Enter.

Recording Investment Sales

When you record the sale of an investment, you describe the transaction by following a series of steps similar to the steps you follow to purchase an investment.

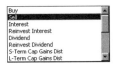

Record a Sale

1 Display the investment account's register.

2 Click New.

3 Enter the sale date.

4 Click the down arrow in the Investment field, and select the name of the stock, bond, or mutual fund you're selling.

5 Click the down arrow in the Activity field, and select Sell from the list.

6 Enter the number of stock or mutual fund shares or the number of individual bonds you're selling.

7 Enter the price per share or price per bond you're receiving.

8 Record the commission you paid to sell the stock, bond, or mutual fund.

9 Verify the contents of the Total field, and edit the value if necessary, to reflect the total purchase amount.

10 Click the down arrow in the Transfer To field, and select the bank account or associated cash account in which you'll deposit the sale proceeds.

11 Click Enter.

If you have more than one lot, Money asks if you want to specify the lot you want to sell. If you indicate that you want to sell a lot other than the first one you bought, click Next to specify the lot.

Recording Dividends and Distributions

Periodically, of course, you'll receive a mutual fund dividend distribution. Many stocks also pay dividends that you will have to record as well.

Record Dividends

1 Display the investment account's register.

2 Click New.

3 Enter the dividend date.

4 Click the down arrow in the Investment field, and select the name of the stock or mutual fund that is distributing the dividend.

5 Click the down arrow in the Activity field, and select an entry from the list. For dividends from stocks, select Dividend.

6 Specify the amount of the dividend.

7 Click the down arrow in the Transfer To field, and select the bank account or associated cash account in which you'll deposit the dividend.

8 Click Enter.

Reinvesting Dividends and Distributions

With a mutual fund, you usually have the option of reinvesting the distributions you receive when the mutual fund returns a profit. By reinvesting, you continue to accumulate more and more shares. Typically, reinvested distributions aren't subject to the same sales commissions that regular purchases are. Some stock companies also offer shareholders the opportunity to buy more shares with their dividends. As with mutual funds, these dividend reinvestment programs, often called DRIPs, let investors add to their holdings at a low cost because they typically don't require a brokerage commission.

TRY THIS

Fill out only the Price and Total fields, and Money calculates the quantity of shares.

Reinvest Dividends or Distributions

1 Display the investment account register.

2 Click New.

3 Enter the reinvestment date.

4 Click the down arrow in the Investment field, and select the name of the investment.

5 Click the down arrow in the Activity field, and select an appropriate entry to describe the reinvestment. Select Reinvest for dividends from stocks.

6 Describe how many mutual fund shares you're purchasing by reinvesting the distribution.

7 Give the price per share you're paying for the new mutual fund shares.

8 Record any commission you paid to purchase the investment.

9 Verify the contents of the Total field, and edit the value, if necessary, so that it correctly reflects the total purchase amount.

10 Click enter.

Select Reinvest Interest for a reinvested interest distribution, select Reinvest Dividend for a reinvested dividend distribution, select Reinvest S-Term CG Dist for a reinvested short-term capital gains distribution, or select Reinvest L-Term CG Dist for a reinvested long-term capital gains distribution.

Recording Other Income and Expenses

Money lets you record other income and expenses that don't fit into named categories. For example, if you have income that can't correctly be categorized as interest, dividends, or capital gains, you use the Other Income category. If you have an investment expense such as a brokerage account fee that you pay to maintain an account, use the Other Expense category.

> **TIP**
>
> *If the income or expense amount is related only to the brokerage account in general, for example, and not to a specific investment, leave the Investment box empty.*

> **TIP**
>
> *If you buy stocks or bonds on margin, you record margin interest—the interest costs that your broker charges you on the borrowed money—as an Other Expense transaction.*

Record Other Income or Expenses

1 Display the investment account register.

2 Click New.

3 Enter the transaction date.

4 Click the down arrow in the Investment field, and select the name of the investment.

5 Click the down arrow in the Activity field, and select either Other Income or Other Expense.

6 Categorize the income or expense amount in the same way you would for a bank account transaction.

7 Enter the income or expense amount.

8 Click the down arrow in the Transfer From or Transfer To field, and select the account into which you'll deposit the income or from which you'll pay the expense.

9 Click Enter.

Recording Stock Splits

Companies whose share prices are growing quickly sometimes split shares of their stock to reduce the price per share. The company then compensates its current investors with additional shares so that they don't lose money. Stock splits don't change the value of your holdings, they just make it easier for people to buy individual shares and even lots because the shares and the lots are less expensive.

TIP

Stock dividends. *A stock dividend is a dividend that is paid in stock. As a practical matter, however, a stock dividend works exactly like a stock split. For example, if a stock pays a dividend equal to one-twentieth of a share, you get 21 new shares for every 20 old ones. Because the market is smart enough to adjust accordingly, this is the same as a 21:20 split.*

Record a Stock Split

1. Display the investment account register.

2. Click Split Shares on the Accounts bar.

3. Click the down arrow in the Investment field, and select the stock that's splitting.

4. Enter the stock split date.

5. Enter the number of new shares you're receiving.

6. Enter the number of old shares you had before the split.

7. Click OK.

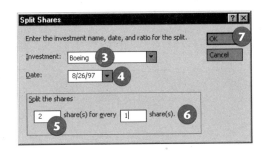

8

Recording Bond Interest

Bonds typically reward their holders by regularly paying interest. You record interest in the same way you record dividends and distributions for stocks and mutual funds.

TIP

Some bonds, such as zero-coupon bonds, don't pay interest over the course of their life. Instead, these bonds pay interest at the very end, when the bond is redeemed. See "Accrued Interest on Bonds" for more information about how to treat zero-coupon bonds.

TIP

Return of capital. *A return of capital is the return of a portion of the price you originally paid. To record a return of capital, or a liquidated dividend, select Return Of Capital from the Activity field. You know that a dividend is a return of capital because the statement you receive with the payment will identify it as such.*

Record Bond Interest

1. Display the investment account register.

2. Click New.

3. Enter the interest payment date.

4. Click the down arrow in the Investment field, and select the name of the bond paying the interest.

5. Click the down arrow in the Activity field, and select Interest.

6. Enter the amount of the interest payment.

7. Click the down arrow in the Transfer To field, and select the bank account or associated cash account in which you'll deposit the interest payment.

8. Click Enter.

Accrued Interest on Bonds

Unless you buy or sell a bond on the interest payment day, some of what you pay when you buy the bond and some of what you receive when you sell it represents accrued interest. Accrued interest is simply the interest the bond has earned since the last interest payment date. Unfortunately, accrued interest increases both the work and the complexity of bond record-keeping.

Accrued Interest on Bonds You Purchase

To record the purchase of a bond with accrued interest, you record two transactions. For example, let's say you just purchased, for $1,020, a $1,000 bond with $20 of accrued interest. First, record the purchase of the actual bond without the accrued interest: $1,000. Then, record a return of capital transaction with a negative return of capital amount equal to the accrued interest (in this case,–$20). At this point, Money shows your bond's value as equal to $1,020.

When you get your next interest payment—let's say it's $60—you record two transactions: a return of capital transaction equal to $20 and an interest income transaction equal to $40. In this way, you don't count as income the $20 of accrued interest you actually paid when you purchased the bond. And you record as interest income only the $40 you actually earned.

Accrued Interest on Bonds You Own

Some bonds accrue interest but don't pay the interest. (The bond issuer typically reports this accrued but unpaid interest on form 1099-OID at the end of the year.) To keep a good record of these bonds, you need to record the accrued interest annually because the interest income is taxable. To do this, you record two transactions. First, you record the accrued bond interest as regular interest income. When you record this transaction, transfer the bond interest income to your associated cash account—even though there really won't be a deposit because the interest will only accrue. Then record a negative return of capital transaction equal to the accrued interest. When you record this second transaction, transfer the bond interest income from your associated cash account. In this way, Money records the interest income and adjusts the bond value for the accrued interest.

8

Bond Premiums and Bond Discounts

If you pay more for a bond than the redemption price, the extra amount you pay is called a premium. You might ask, why would you and other investors pay more for a bond than the borrower will pay to redeem it? Because the borrower agrees to pay a higher rate of interest than the current rate. For example, imagine that a borrower issues $1,000 bonds that pay 6.6 percent interest, or $66. Subsequent to the issue of the bonds, investors like you decide that 6 percent is the going bond interest rate; a bond that pays $66 is therefore worth more than $1,000 because $66 is 6 percent of $1,100, not $1,000.

Bond premiums present an accounting problem. In effect, the $100 is an expense, or loss. Why? Although you might pay $1,100 for the bond described in the preceding paragraph, you only receive $1,000 when you redeem it.

For record-keeping purposes, you should spread the expense of the $100 bond premium over the years until the borrower redeems the bond. This is called amortization. To amortize the bond premium, multiply the effective interest rate the bond earns by its purchase price, and then subtract this amount from the actual interest the bond pays during the year. The difference is the bond premium expense that you will record the first year.

In the years that follow, you make only one minor modification in this bond-premium allocation formula. Instead of multiplying the effective interest rate the bond earns by the bond purchase price, you multiply the effective interest rate by the bond purchase price minus the bond premium amounts that you've already allocated.

Suppose, for example, that you purchase a $1,050 bond that pays an effective interest rate, or yield to maturity, of 6 percent. Further suppose that the bond pays $66 in interest annually. Given these facts, the bond premium charged as expense the first year would be calculated like this:

$$\$66 - (6\% \times \$1,050) = \$3$$

During the second year, the bond premium that is charged as an expense would be calculated as follows:

$$\$66 - [6\% \times (\$1,050 - \$3)] = \$3.18$$

During the third year, the bond premium charged as an expense would be calculated like so:

$$\$66 - [6\% \times (\$1,050 - \$3 - \$3.18)] = \$3.56$$

To record the allocations of bond premiums as expenses, you record two transactions. Record the bond premium allocation as an Other Expense for the bond, and specify the Transfer From account as the associated cash account. Record a return of capital transaction equal to the bond premium allocation, and specify the Transfer To account as the associated cash account.

Handling Bond Discounts

Bond discounts arise when buyers pay less for a bond than its redemption price. The difference between the purchase price and the redemption price is called the discount. A discount indicates that the borrower is paying less than the current rate.

Accounting for bond discounts works much like accounting for bond premiums. Suppose, for example, that a borrower issues a $1,000 bond that pays 6 percent interest, or $60, and that subsequent to the issue, investors decide that 6.66 percent should be the going rate. In this case, a bond that pays $60 is worth less than $1,000, because $60 is 6.66 percent of $900, not $1,000.

The $100 difference is income because, although you might pay $900 for the bond described in the preceding paragraph, you'll receive $1,000 when you redeem it. You should treat the $100 bond discount you receive as income and spread it over the years between the purchase and the redemption.

To make this discount allocation, you multiply the effective interest rate the bond earns by the bond purchase price and then subtract from this figure the actual interest the bond paid for the year. The difference is the bond discount income you record for the year. The effective interest rate is simply the yield to maturity—a figure you'll obtain when you purchase the bond.

In following years, you modify this bond-discount allocation formula by multiplying the effective interest rate by the bond purchase price plus the bond discount amounts already allocated.

Suppose that you purchase a $950 bond that pays an effective interest rate of 6.5 percent. This bond annually pays $60 in interest. Given these facts, the bond discount allocated as income the first year would be calculated like this:

$$(6.5\% \times \$950) - \$60 = \$1.75$$

During the second year, the bond discount allocated as income would be calculated as follows:

$$[6.5\% \times (\$950 + \$1.75)] - \$60 = \$1.86$$

During the third year, the bond discount allocated as income would be calculated like so:

$$[6.5\% \times (\$950 + \$1.75 + \$1.86)] - \$60 = \$1.98$$

To record the allocations of bond discounts as income, you treat the bond discount as accrued interest—which, in fact, is what it is. To do this, you first record the accrued bond interest (the bond discount allocation) as regular interest income. When you record this transaction, transfer the bond interest income to your associated cash account, even though there really won't be a deposit. (The interest will only accrue.) Then record a negative return of capital transaction equal to the accrued interest. When you record this second transaction, transfer the bond interest income out of your associated cash account. In this way, Money records the interest income and adjusts the bond value for the accrued interest.

9

Real Estate Investing

Many investors prize real estate because it is a hedge against inflation and because many types of real estate investments deliver solid cash returns. Real estate investments present unusual record-keeping challenges, however. Recording the income and expenses of passive real estate investments (such as limited partnership units or shares and real estate investment trusts or REITs) is more complicated than, say, recording the income and expenses that pertain to stocks or bonds. (Don't worry if you don't understand this lingo yet—I'll go into more detail in a minute.) Active real estate investments, such as rental income properties, require you to set up business bookkeeping systems. In spite of these challenges, however, Microsoft Money provides real estate investors with a wonderful set of tools and possibilities.

Creating Passive Real Estate Investment Accounts

Passive real estate investments include limited partnership units and shares in real estate investment trusts. At first glance, these investments resemble stocks, but they actually work quite differently because not all of the cash you receive comes in the form of interest or dividends. Typically, a substantial portion of the distributions from a passive real estate investment represents a return of capital. In spite of their complexity, however, you can use Money to keep accurate financial records of passive real estate investments.

Real Estate Investment Trust

Set Up a Passive Real Estate Investment Account

1 Click Accounts on the navigation bar once or twice to display the Account Manager window.

2 Click the New Account button.

3 Optionally, enter the name of the financial institution associated with the account, and click Next.

4 Select Investment from the list of accounts, and click Next.

5 Enter a name for the investment account, and click Next.

6 Specify whether or not the account is tax deferred by selecting the appropriate option, and click Next.

7 Enter the estimated value of the real estate investments in the account.

8 Specify whether or not the account has an associated cash account, and click Next.

The best way to start investing in real estate.
Invest in your own home. On average, home ownership investment has delivered returns roughly equal to those of the stock market. Note, however, that it's difficult to make money on any real estate investment—including the purchase of a home—unless you hold the investment for a lengthy period of time. Typically, you need several years of appreciation just to pay for the selling costs.

9 If the account does have an associated cash account, enter the cash account's ending balance from your last monthly statement, and click Next.

10 Specify in general terms how you use the real estate investment account, and click Next.

11 If a financial institution is associated with the account, Money asks if you have any other accounts to set up. Click the I Have No Other Accounts At This Bank option button, and click Next.

12 If Money asks if you want to set up online banking for the account, click the No, Not Now option button and then click Finish.

9

Recording Real Estate Investment Purchases

Whenever you purchase partnership units or shares in a real estate investment trust, you need to describe the purchase in the investment account's Account Register window. The process of recording a passive real estate investment purchase is the same as the process you go through to record a stock, bond, or mutual fund purchase.

Record a Passive Real Estate Investment Purchase

1. Display the investment account register.

2. Click New.

3. Enter the purchase date.

4. Enter a name for the investment. If you haven't purchased units or shares of the real estate partnership or investment trust before, Money displays the Create New Investment dialog box.

5. Click the Stock option button, click Next, and then click Finish.

6. Click the down arrow in the Activity field, and select Buy from the list.

7. Enter the number of partnership units or trust shares you're purchasing.

8. Enter the price per unit or share you're paying.

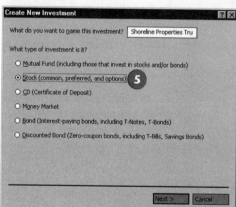

Passive real estate investments. *In a passive real estate investment, you don't actively manage the investment. For example, you don't pick a property manager, collect rent, or arrange financing. If you purchased shares of a real estate investment trust (REIT) or invested in a real estate project as a limited partner, your investment is probably passive.*

If you're describing a publicly traded real estate investment and you intend to use Money's Online Quotes feature, you need to enter the security symbol in the Create New Investment dialog box. Refer to Section 10 for more information about Online Quotes.

9 Record any sales commission you paid.

10 Verify the contents of the Total field, and edit the value, if necessary, so that it correctly reflects the total purchase amount.

11 Click the down arrow in the Transfer From field, and select the bank account or associated cash account you're using to purchase the investment. Keep this box blank if you're recording a past purchase.

12 Click Enter.

Recording Real Estate Investment Sales

When you sell units or shares of a real estate investment, of course, you describe that transaction too. You record the sale of a real estate investment in the same way that you record the sale of a stock or mutual fund shares or individual bonds.

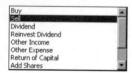

Record a Real Estate Investment Sale

1 Display the investment account register, and click New.

2 Enter the sale date.

3 Identify the name of the real estate investment you're selling.

4 Click the down arrow in the Activity field, and select Sell from the list.

5 Describe how many partnership units or trust shares you're selling.

6 Enter the price per share or per unit you're receiving.

7 Record any sales commission you paid to sell the units or shares.

8 Verify the contents of the Total field, and edit the value, if necessary, to correctly reflect the total purchase amount.

9 Click the down arrow in the Transfer To field, and select the bank account or associated cash account in which you'll deposit the sale proceeds.

10 Click Enter.

Recording Real Estate Investment Distributions

At the end of the quarter or the end of the year, you usually receive a real estate investment fund dividend distribution which you then need to record.

TIP

Select Interest for an interest distribution, Dividend for a dividend distribution, S-Term Cap Gains Dist for a short-term capital gains distribution, L-Term Cap Gains for a long-term capital gains distribution, or Other Income.

TIP

The quarterly or year-end distribution statement you receive identifies the type of distribution. You don't have to worry about making this determination.

Record a Real Estate Investment Distribution

1. Display the investment account register and click New.

2. Enter the distribution date.

3. Click the down arrow in the Investment field, and select the investment fund making the distribution.

4. Click the down arrow in the Activity field, and select an entry from the list.

5. Specify the amount of the distribution.

6. Click the down arrow in the Transfer To field, and select the bank account or associated cash account in which you'll deposit the distribution.

7. Click Enter to record the distribution.

Recording Return of Capital Transactions

Sometimes a distribution isn't a share of the real estate profits but a return of capital—a return of a portion of the price you originally paid. Recording a return of capital for real estate investments works the same way as it does for stocks and bonds.

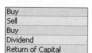

Record a Return of Capital Transaction

1 Display the investment account register.

2 Click New.

3 Enter the return of capital date.

4 Click the down arrow in the Investment field, and select the investment.

5 Click the down arrow in the Activity field, and select Return Of Capital from the list.

6 Enter the amount of the capital return.

7 Click the down arrow in the Transfer To field, and select the bank account or associated cash account in which you'll deposit the return of capital.

8 Click Enter.

Setting Up Real Estate Property Accounts

If you're an active real estate investor, you can also use Money to simplify and expedite your record-keeping. In essence, you'll use Money to track three things: the adjusted cost basis of your properties, the mortgages associated with any of your properties, and the income and expenses that individual properties produce. To track the adjusted cost basis of your investments, you must first set up asset accounts for each individual property you own.

SEE ALSO

For information about choosing a mortgage and making refinancing decisions, see page 98.

Set Up an Active Real Estate Investment Account

1 Click Accounts on the navigation bar once or twice to display the Account Manager window.

2 Click the New Account button.

3 Leave the Bank Or Financial Institution field empty, and click Next.

4 Select Asset from the list of accounts, and click Next.

5 Enter a name for the asset account, and click Next.

6 Enter the original purchase price of the property.

7 Money asks whether or not a loan is associated with the investment. Select the appropriate option, and click Finish.

Building a Real Estate Investment Category List

To keep records of an individual property's income and expenses, you do two very simple things. First create a list of categories specifically for tracking your real estate investments. Next you use these real estate income and expense categories to record transactions related to your real estate investments.

TIP

Although you can use any list of income or expense categories you want, you should base your categories on Schedule E of the federal income tax form, which you use to report your real estate profits or losses to the federal government.

Add a Real Estate Income or Expense Category

1 Click Categories on the navigation bar.

2 Click the New button.

3 Click the Create A New Category option button, and click Next.

4 Enter a name for the new real estate category.

5 Specify whether the new category is an income or expense category by selecting the appropriate option, and then click Next.

6 Select a general group to describe the new category from the list, and click Finish.

7 Repeat steps 2 through 6 to add each of the income and expense categories you need.

Setting Up Property Classifications

If you own more than one piece of property, you'll also want to create classifications to track each property's income and expenses. To create property classifications, you need to first turn on the classification feature and then you need to create a classification for each property you own.

TIP

Once you create a Properties classification, the Properties field shows up in the transaction forms for all of your asset, bank, and cash accounts.

TRY THIS

You may want to use a property's street address as its classification name.

Turn on the Classification Feature

1. Click Categories on the navigation bar.

2. Click the Classification 1 button. Money displays the Add Classification dialog box.

3. Click the Properties option button.

4. Click OK.

Create Property Classifications

1. Click Categories on the navigation bar.

2. Click the Properties tab.

3. Click the New button.

4. Enter the name of the real estate investment.

5. Click OK.

Tracking the Adjusted Cost of Property

Once you set up an asset account, you can use it to track improvements you make to the property (because improvements increase the property's adjusted cost) and your annual depreciation (because depreciation decreases the property's adjusted cost). The adjusted cost basis of a property is important. When you someday sell the property, you calculate the capital gain or loss by subtracting the adjusted cost from the net sales price.

TIP

The tax laws treat various types of property differently when it comes to depreciation. How you depreciate a real estate property also depends on the tax laws in effect the year you placed the property into service. If you want to know how much depreciation to use in a given year's profit calculation, consult with a tax advisor or contact the Internal Revenue Service for help.

Record Depreciation

1. Display the real estate property's asset account register.

2. Click the Decrease tab, and if necessary, click New.

3. Enter the date for the asset depreciation transaction.

4. Optionally, enter a description of the asset depreciation in the Pay To field.

5. Enter the amount of the annual depreciation charge.

6. Enter Depreciation in the Category field. If you have not recorded depreciation before, Money displays the New Category dialog box. Enter a description of the category, and click Enter.

7. Classify the real estate investment in the Properties field.

8. Click Enter.

Record a Capital Improvement

1. Display the register for the bank account or associated cash account you'll use to pay for the capital improvements.

2. Click the Check tab, and if necessary, click New.

3. Enter the check number.

4. Enter the check date.

5. Enter the name of the person or business you're paying.

6. Enter the check amount.

7. Click the down arrow in the Category field, and select Transfer from the list.

8. Click the down arrow in the Subcategory field, and select the name of the property account.

9. Classify the real estate investment in the Properties field.

10. Enter a memo describing the improvement in detail.

11. Click Enter.

Recording Real Estate Income and Expense Transactions

After you've created a list of income and expense categories, keep your checkbook as usual—except when you record an income or expense related to a real estate property. Then you use the appropriate real estate income or expense category and describe the real estate investment using the Properties fields.

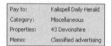

Pay to:	Kalispell Daily Herald
Category:	Miscellaneous
Properties:	43 Devonshire
Memo:	Classified advertising

Record Real Estate Income

1 Display the register for the bank account or associated cash account in which you want to deposit the real estate income.

2 Click the Deposit tab, and if necessary, click New.

3 Enter the check number.

4 Enter the deposit date.

5 Enter the name of the person or business who paid you.

6 Enter the amount of the check.

7 Click the down arrow in the Category field, and select a real estate income category that describes the deposit.

8 Click the down arrow in the Properties field, and select the real estate property's classification.

9 Click Enter.

SEE ALSO

For more information on using bank accounts, see Section 3.

Record Real Estate Expense

1. Display the register for the bank account or associated cash account from which you want to pay for the real estate expense.

2. Click the Check tab, and if necessary, click New.

3. Enter the check number.

4. Enter the date.

5. Enter the name of the person or business you're paying.

6. Enter the amount of the check.

7. Click the down arrow in the Category field, and select a real estate expense category that describes the expenditure.

8. Click the down arrow in the Properties field, and select the real estate property's classification.

9. Click Enter.

Reporting on Active Real Estate Investments

Once you collect income and expense data for active real estate investments, it is easy to create a report that summarizes income and expense data by property.

TRY THIS

Use this Income vs. Spending report to get most of the data you need to complete the Schedule E form.

Produce Real Estate Investment Report

1. Click Reports on the navigation bar.

2. Click the Spending Habits button.

3. Select Income vs. Spending from the Spending Habits list.

4. Click the Go To Report/ Chart button.

5. Click the Customize button to display the Customize Report dialog box.

6. Click the down arrow in the Columns field, and select Properties from the list.

7. Click View to update the Income vs. Spending report using different columns to show income and spending by real estate investment.

Online Banking, Bill Payment, and Investing

One way to take advantage of the power of emerging online technologies is by using any or all of Microsoft Money's online services:

◆ Online Bill Payment

◆ Online Banking

◆ Online Quotes

◆ The MoneyZone

You might have read an article or two about home banking and how it will revolutionize the way people interact with their banks. More and more banks now offer some sort of online services. Users of version 3 of Microsoft Money had only three banks in the entire country to choose from if they wanted to bank online. Now more than 20 banks participate, including some of the largest in the country.

You can sign up for any or all of Money's online services. The services are tightly integrated into the program and require no additional software. To use all four of the services, however, you do need a modem. To use online banking, you also need an account at a participating bank, and to use the MoneyZone, you need a web browser and Internet access as well.

Setting Up Online Services

Once you have a modem installed and working properly, you can set up online services in Money. With Online Banking, you can download your bank statements and transactions and transfer money between online accounts. With Online Bill Payment, you can send checks electronically.

Online Checking

SEE ALSO

If you haven't yet created the account for which you want to use Money's online services, see page 16 for more information about creating bank accounts.

Set Up Online Banking or Bill Payment

1. Click Online Banking on the navigation bar.

2. Click Getting Started on the Online bar.

3. To find out what online services your bank offers and to get the prerequisite information about setting up online banking with your bank, go through steps 2, 3, and 4 by clicking the buttons and following the directions.

4. Once you have activated an online account with your bank and have received an information packet from them, click the Set Up Online Services button and click Next to begin setting up online services in Money.

5. Click the Yes, I Have This Information option button, and click Next.

6. Enter the personal information Money requests, and click Next twice.

7. Select the first account you want to use for online services in the Account field, and click Next.

TIP

Once you set up online services for an account, a lightning bolt icon appears next to the account in the list of accounts and in the Account Manager window.

TIP

About online safety. *Online services are actually safer to use than ATM machines. There are only a couple of safety precautions you should take. Choose a password that can't easily be guessed and can't be found in a dictionary. For example, don't use your birthday, address, or phone number, regardless of how easy it is for you to remember such a password. The best passwords combine two disparate facts, for instance the name of your favorite restaurant and the number of your favorite athlete. Second, change your password periodically. And of course, don't share your password with others or write it down near your computer.*

8 Check the boxes next to the services the account is approved for, and click Next.

9 Enter your account number and bank routing and ID numbers, and click Next.

10 If you have more accounts to set up, click the Yes, I Want To Set Up Another Account option button and click Next to continue setting up your other accounts for online services. Otherwise, click the No option button, and click Finish.

10

Making Electronic Payments

With Money's Online Bill Payment service, you can pay any business or individual in the United States right from your computer. The service works with any checking account in the United States, and the suggested retail price is $4.95 per month for 20 payments. Additional payments are usually about $.50 each.

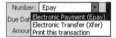

Enter an Electronic Payment

1. Display the register for the account you've set up for online services.

2. Click the Check tab, and click New, if necessary.

3. Click the down arrow in the Number field, and select Epay from the list.

4. Enter the date you want the payment delivered (or the payment's due date).

5. Enter the name of the payee. This name will appear on the envelope and the Pay To line of the check. If you've never made out a check to this payee, Money will display the Online Payee Details box asking you for the payee's address.

6. Make sure this is the way you want the payee's name to appear on the check and the envelope.

7. Enter the address including the 5- or 9-digit zip code of the payee. Use the second line of the street address field, if necessary.

TIP

You only have to enter information once for each payee.

TIP

If you have created an electronic payment but have not yet sent it to the Online Bill Payment service, Money displays a reminder on the Money Home Screen and in the account register.

TIP

Once you enter a transaction, an open envelope icon and a lighting bolt icon appear in the Number field of the account register. The lightning bolt means that it's an electronic payment. The open envelope means that you haven't sent the payment yet.

8 Optionally, enter the phone number of the payee. Although this is not required, it is a good idea in case there is a problem with the payment.

9 If the payment is going to a business with which you have an account, such as the phone company, enter your account number.

10 Click OK to return to the register.

11 Enter the amount of the payment.

12 Categorize the payment as you normally would.

13 Enter a memo.

14 Click Enter.

10

Sending Electronic Payments

Once you enter all your electronic payments, the next step is to send them to the online services. Then the check is cut so that it can be sent through the mail to the payee.

Reminders
You have the following things to do:

Online Banking...

TRY THIS

If you have an electronic payment entered but not yet sent and you're in the account register, you can click Online Banking on the Accounts bar to go to Online Banking and send the payment.

TIP

Use the Dialing Properties dialog box to disable call waiting or to enter a number to access an outside line.

Send an Electronic Payment

1 Click Online Banking on the navigation bar.

2 Click Connect on the Online bar, and review the payment information you entered. If you subscribe to the Online Banking service, you'll also see instructions for updating the statement and balance of your Online Banking accounts.

3 Click the Connect button.

4 Enter your PIN number.

5 Optionally, click the Dialing Properties button to customize the way in which Windows handles your calls.

6 Click the Connect button to send the payment instructions. You'll see a progression of messages as your payments are sent and received.

7 Confirm that the transaction was completed in the Call Summary dialog box, and click Close.

Cancel an Electronic Payment

1 Display the account register with the electronic payment you want to cancel.

2 Right-click the transaction you want to cancel, and choose the shortcut menu's Mark As command and the Mark As submenu's Void command.

3 Click the Yes option button when Money asks whether or not you want to create an instruction to cancel the payment.

4 Click Online Banking on the navigation bar.

5 Click Connect on the Online bar, and make sure the cancel payment instruction is there.

6 Click the Connect button to send the cancellation instruction to the bank.

10

Making Automatic Payments

If you want to take the convenience of online bill payment one step further, you can also tell the Online Bill Payment service to make payments for you automatically. This only works for recurring payments of a fixed amount, such as rent, car, and mortgage payments. When you authorize an automatic payment, the checks are sent weekly, monthly, bimonthly, or at whatever frequency you specify.

TIP

Be careful with automatic payments, because once you set them up, the payments are made whether or not you connect to the online services.

Create an Automatic Payment

1. Click Bills on the navigation bar.

2. Click the New Bill button.

3. Click the Bill option button, and click Next twice.

4. Click the down arrow in the Frequency field, and select a payment frequency from the list.

5. Click the down arrow in the Number field, and select Automatic Payment (Apay) from the list.

6. Select the name of the account from which you want the payments to be made. The account must be set up with the Online Bill Payment service.

7. Enter the date you want the first payment to be made.

8. Enter the name of the person or business you're paying.

9. Enter the payment amount.

10. Click OK.

11 Enter the number of payments or the date of the final payment. If you want payments to be made until you cancel them, leave both fields empty.

12 Click OK. If this is a new payee, fill in the boxes of the Online Payee Details dialog box and click OK.

13 Click Online Banking on the navigation bar.

14 Click Connect on the Online bar, and review the Automatic Payment information.

15 Click the Connect button to send the payment.

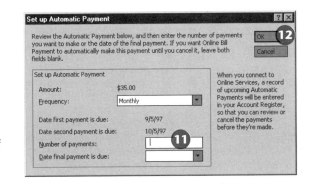

10

Canceling Automatic Payments

You have two options for canceling an automatic payment. You can cancel an individual occurrence of the payment but keep the automatic payment in your payment calendar for the future, or you can delete all occurrences of the payment.

TIP

You can also delete and individual automatic payment from within the Bills area by right-clicking the automatic payment and choosing the shortcut menu's Delete Only This Instance command.

Cancel an Individual Automatic Payment

1 In the online account's register, right-click the transaction you want to cancel.

2 Choose the shortcut menu's Mark As command, and then choose the Mark As submenu's Void command.

3 Click Online Banking on the navigation bar.

4 Click Connect on the Online bar, and review the cancel payment instructions.

5 Click the Connect button to send the instruction.

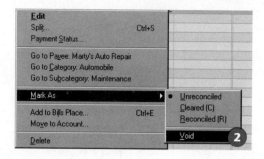

TIP

To make sure you have accurate records of your automatic payments, connect to online services at least once a month.

Permanently Cancel an Automatic Payment

1 Click Bills on the navigation bar.

2 Right-click the automatic payment you want to cancel, and choose Delete All Instances from the shortcut menu.

3 Click Online Banking on the navigation bar.

4 Click Connect on the Online bar, and review the instructions to cancel the automatic payment.

5 Click the Connect button.

Edit
Enter Only This One

Go to Account: Online Checking
Go to Payee: West Coast Telephone
Go to Category: Bills
Go to Subcategory: Telephone

Delete Only This Instance
Delete All Instances   **2**

10

Downloading Bank Account Records

Before you can use online banking services, you must have an account set up at a participating bank. Then once you're set up, you can easily download statements from your bank, transfer money between accounts, and even order new checks. Downloading your statements is a cinch. It involves two steps: downloading the records and adding the downloaded transactions to your account register.

TIP

You can find out which banks in your area participate in Money's Online Banking service by accessing the MoneyZone. (See page 154.)

Download Bank Account Records

1. Click Online Banking on the navigation bar.

2. Click Connect on the Online bar.

3. Click the Connect button.

4. Enter your PIN number.

5. Optionally, click the Dialing Properties button to customize the way in which Windows handles your calls.

6. Click the Connect button. You'll see a series of messages as your computer sends and then receives information.

7. Confirm that the call was completed in the Call Summary dialog box, and click Close.

Add Downloaded Transactions to the Account Register

1 Click Statements & Balances on the Online bar.

2 Select an account from the list, and click the Read Statement button.

3 Click the Update Account Register button.

4 For each transaction, Money tries to find a matching transaction in your account register. When it finds one that appears to match, you then confirm whether this is the same transaction or ask Money to keep looking.

5 If Money doesn't find a match for a transaction, it displays the transaction and gives you a chance to make any changes. At this point, you might want to change the payee name or add a category or subcategory.

6 Make any changes you want to each downloaded transaction, and click Next to move on to the next one.

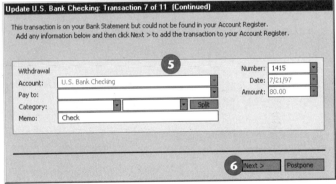

10

Transferring Money Online

As long as you have two accounts at the same bank and both are registered for the Online Banking Service, you can electronically transfer money between them.

TIP

For electronic transfers, you must use today's date. The transfer takes place at the end of the day. If you request an electronic transfer after the cut-off time, it is processed at the end of the following business day. Transfers to and from credit card accounts have an additional one-day delay.

TRY THIS

Check your statement on the day following the transfer to make sure the money was transferred.

Transfer Money Between Accounts

1. Display the register for the online account you want to transfer money from.

2. Click the Transfer tab.

3. Click the down arrow in the Number field, and select Electronic Transfer (Xfer) from the list.

4. Click the down arrow in the From field, and select the name of the account from which you're transferring the money.

5. Enter the transfer date.

6. Click the down arrow in the To field, and select the name of the account to which you're transferring money.

7. Enter the amount you want transferred between the accounts.

8. Click Enter.

9. Click Online Banking on the navigation bar.

10. Click Connect on the Online bar and review the transfer instructions.

11. Click the Connect button.

Sending E-Mail to Your Bank

You can send electronic mail to your bank to inquire about a payment, request a copy of a check, order new paper checks, or send a general purpose letter.

Write Letter...

TRY THIS

Click Contact Information on the Online bar to see your bank's contact information.

TIP

To delete a letter you have written, right-click the letter from the list of transactions to send and choose the shortcut menu's Remove command.

Send an E-Mail to Your Bank

1 Click Online Banking on the navigation bar.

2 Click the Write Letter button.

3 Select the option that corresponds with the type of letter you want to send, and click Continue.

4 Write the letter.

5 Click OK.

6 Click Connect to send the letter.

10

Online Quotes

With Money's Online Quotes service, you can download the latest prices of a stock or major mutual fund and, in so doing, automatically update your investment portfolio. The service costs $2.95 per month for six sessions. Additional downloads cost $.50 each. If you track a lot of stocks, you'll find that this service can save you time searching through the newspaper. Another advantage of the Online Quotes service for serious investors is that stock prices are updated every 15 minutes.

TIP

If you don't know the official, market-approved symbol for a stock or mutual fund, call your stockbroker or check your local paper and see if it's listed there. In stock tables, it's often listed under the heading "Ticker."

TIP

If you want to track stocks you don't actually own, click New in the Investment Portfolio window and click the A New Investment option button.

Enter Market Symbols for Stocks and Mutual Funds

1 Click Investments on the navigation bar.

2 Select the investment, and click the Go To button.

3 Enter the symbol or click Find Symbol to use Microsoft Investor to find the symbol.

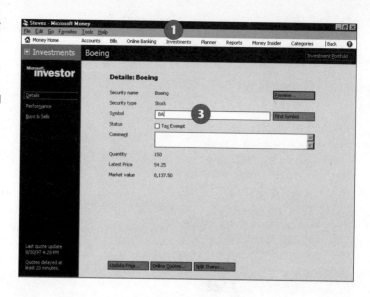

If you don't have an account with an Internet service provider, select Subscription Quotes and sign up for the service by filling out the application Money provides.

Download Market Prices

1 Click Investments on the navigation bar.

2 Click the Online Quotes button.

3 If you have never used Online Quotes before, select an Online Quotes service from the drop-down list box and click Next.

4 Select the country you're calling from and click Next.

5 Review the investments for which you've entered market-approved symbols. If you don't want to update one or more of the investments, clear the check box.

6 Click the Call button. You'll see a series of messages as your computer sends and receives information.

7 Click Update Price to update the prices in your Investment Portfolio.

8 Enter the current price in the Price text box and click Update.

9 Click Close to close the Update Price dialog box.

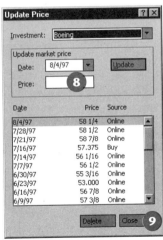

10

Researching Investments on the Internet

The Internet is the richest source of investment and other personal financial information. Unfortunately, it's also the most disorganized. There isn't a single place to go to get all the information you want. You can get investment information from newsgroups, from mailing list messages, and on World Wide Web sites.

I'm not going to describe how to use all these features here because the procedure differs depending on your Internet service provider, on the web browser you use, and on your e-mail client software. For purposes of this discussion, therefore, I assume you already have access to the Internet. So in this section, I'll tell you specifically where to locate investing and personal finance information.

A Review of Available Newsgroups

An Internet *newsgroup* is really just an electronic bulletin board. Some people post messages on the bulletin board, and other people read them. A handful of newsgroups post messages on personal financial topics. As long as you have a newsgroup reader and access to the Internet or subscribe to an online service that provides access to newsgroups, you can read the posted messages and even post your own.

At the time I am writing this, the following newsgroups are available and active enough to warrant at least a quick review.

NEWSGROUP NAME	WHAT IT COVERS
misc.invest	All types of investment discussion
misc.invest.canada	Investments in Canada or of special interest to Canadians
misc.invest.funds	Mutual fund investing
misc.invest.real-estate	Real estate investing
misc.invest.stocks	Common stock investments
misc.invest.technical	Technical analysis (charting) of securities

A Review of Available Mailing Lists

Internet *mailing lists* are simply lists of electronic mail addresses. When someone mails a message to the mailing list, everyone whose name is on the list gets the message. This might seem like much ado about nothing, but because mailing lists cater to the interests of their members, mailing lists are powerful communication tools. Several Internet mailing lists provide useful investment information.

MAILING LIST NAME	WHAT IT COVERS AND HOW TO SUBSCRIBE
Persfin-digest	Answers general personal finance questions. Send an e-mail message to *majordomo@shore.net*. Enter your message text as follows: *subscribe persfin-digest*.
Timely Investment Information	Provides a weekly economic update and recommends individual stocks. Send an e-mail message to bobbose@ stockresearch.com. Type the word *Subscribe* on the Subject line and leave the message body blank.

Reviewing World Wide Web Sites

The Internet provides hundreds of popular World Wide Web sites related to personal finance and investing, but one site I recommend that you view is that of the *Wall Street Journal:*

http://update.wsj.com/

Let me quickly mention one other really useful Web site. The *http://www.yahoo.com/* Web site is an index of other Web pages. You can use this site to build a list of investment-related Web pages by typing the word *investing* in the Search text box.

Your Online Service Provider

In a general sense, online services such as America Online, CompuServe, Prodigy, and The Microsoft Network work the same way. Each provides up-to-the-minute news and delayed stock prices, special online columns and newsletters that cover personal financial topics, and personal financial chat rooms and bulletin boards where you can ask questions about investing. Most of the services also let you connect to online brokerage services such as the PC Financial Network.

Compared to haphazardly searching the web, these online services provide a unique advantage. Usually, you can simply click a button and the service displays a list of the personal financial or investing features it provides. The service often also lets you designate or customize your start page to list your investments.

10

The MoneyZone

The MoneyZone is a great way to quickly access technical support with Money and get the latest product information and tips for Money users. From the MoneyZone, you can also link to a wealth of personal finance resources and even send Microsoft Corporation any comments or suggestions you have for improving the program.

TIP

You can also access the MoneyZone directly from your web browser. Just connect to your online service and open your web browser, and then enter the address www.microsoft.com/MoneyZone/.

TIP

Your screen will look a little different from the figure on this page because the MoneyZone page is constantly being updated.

Access the MoneyZone

1 Choose the Help menu's Microsoft On The Web command and the Microsoft On The Web submenu's Microsoft Money Home Page command.

2 Click one of the hyperlinks to access the information you're looking for.

Click here for hints and tips for using Money.

Click here to find out which banks in your area support Online Banking with Money.

Managing a Small Business with Money

Although Microsoft Money is chiefly a personal finance program, it is also perfectly suited for keeping financial records for many small businesses. Before you start using Money for small business accounting, however, you need to think about whether Money will work for you. Here's a breakdown of what Money can and cannot do. Use this list to determine whether Money will meet your needs or if you should instead upgrade to a complete small business accounting program.

Tasks you can complete with Money:

- ◆ Print checks for a business
- ◆ Track business bank accounts and business investments
- ◆ Prepare payroll for salaried employees

Tasks beyond the scope of Money:

- ◆ Print business forms such as invoices
- ◆ Track inventory, accounts payable accounts, and loans payable accounts
- ◆ Calculate payroll expenses, depreciation, and bid amounts.
- ◆ Track owners equity.

Adding Business Income and Expense Categories

Before you can start keeping your books with Money, you need to have set up the bank account in which you'll make business transactions. Then you need to create categories to track your business income and expenses. Although you can create your own categories, you will want to use the categories that are on the Schedule C business tax return.

TIP

If you're using the same category list to track business and personal expenses, you may want to start each category name with the word Business or the abbreviation Bus to identify it as a business category.

SEE ALSO

For more information about how to specify which tax form and line you want Money to associate with a category, see pages 82–83.

Add an Income or Expense Category

1. Click Categories on the navigation bar

2. Click the New button.

3. Click the Create A New Category option button, and click Next.

4. Enter a name for the business income or expense category.

5. Specify whether the new category is an income or an expense category by selecting the appropriate option, and then click Next.

6. Select a group from the list that best describes the category.

7. Click Finish.

8. Repeat steps 2 through 7 to add all of the business income and business expense categories you need.

Schedule C Categories

The following figure shows the standard business income and expense categories used by sole proprietors to report their profits to the Internal Revenue Service.

Part I — Income

1	Gross receipts or sales. **Caution:** *If this income was reported to you on Form W-2 and the "Statutory employee" box on that form was checked, see page C-2 and check here* ▶ ☐	1
2	Returns and allowances	2
3	Subtract line 2 from line 1	3
4	Cost of goods sold (from line 42 on page 2)	4
5	**Gross profit.** Subtract line 4 from line 3	5
6	Other income, including Federal and state gasoline or fuel tax credit or refund (see page C-2)	6
7	**Gross income.** Add lines 5 and 6 ▶	7

Part II — Expenses. Enter expenses for business use of your home **only** on line 30.

8	Advertising	8	19	Pension and profit-sharing plans	19
9	Bad debts from sales or services (see page C-3)	9	20	Rent or lease (see page C-4):	
10	Car and truck expenses (see page C-3)	10	a	Vehicles, machinery, and equipment	20a
11	Commissions and fees	11	b	Other business property	20b
12	Depletion	12	21	Repairs and maintenance	21
13	Depreciation and section 179 expense deduction (not included in Part III) (see page C-3)	13	22	Supplies (not included in Part III)	22
14	Employee benefit programs (other than on line 19)	14	23	Taxes and licenses	23
15	Insurance (other than health)	15	24	Travel, meals, and entertainment:	
16	Interest:		a	Travel	24a
a	Mortgage (paid to banks, etc.)	16a	b	Meals and entertainment	
b	Other	16b	c	Enter 50% of line 24b subject to limitations (see page C-4)	
17	Legal and professional services	17	d	Subtract line 24c from line 24b	24d
18	Office expense	18	25	Utilities	25
			26	Wages (less employment credits)	26
			27	Other expenses (from line 48 on page 2)	27

Income Categories

Gross receipts or sales
Returns and allowances
Other income

Expense Categories

Advertising
Bad debts
Car and truck expenses
Commissions and fees
Cost of goods sold
Depletion
Depreciation
Employee benefit programs
Insurance
Legal and professional services
Meals and entertainment
Mortgage interest
Office expense
Other interest
Pension and profit-sharing plans
Rent on vehicles, machinery, and equipment
Rent on other business property
Repairs and maintenance
Supplies
Taxes and licenses
Travel
Utilities
Wages
Other expenses

11

Recording Business Income and Expenses

Once you set up the accounts and categories you need for tracking business income and expenses, you're ready to begin recording the income and expenses.

Business

SEE ALSO

For more information about creating an account, see page 16.

Record Business Income

1. Display the business account's register.

2. Click the Deposit tab, and if necessary, click New.

3. Enter the invoice number if applicable.

4. Enter the deposit date.

5. Enter the customer's name, or select the name from the From field.

6. Enter the amount of the deposit.

7. Click the down arrow in the Category field, and select the category that describes the deposit's income category.

8. Optionally, enter a description of the deposit.

9. Click Enter.

SEE ALSO

For a list of data-entry tricks you can use to speed the process of entering transactions into an account register, see page 24.

Record a Business Expense

1. Display the business account's register.

2. Click the Check tab, and if necessary, click New.

3. Enter the check number.

4. Enter the check date.

5. Enter the name of the person or business you're paying, or select it from the Pay To field.

6. Enter the amount of the check.

7. Click the down arrow in the Category field, and select the category that describes the check's expense category.

8. Optionally, enter a description of the check.

9. Click Enter.

Preparing for Accounts Receivable Accounting

Although Money isn't really set up to invoice customers and to track the amounts that you've billed to and collected from customers, with a little coercion, you can use Money to keep track of invoices and payments. You just need to set up an accounts receivable account and then use a word processing program to produce the actual invoice.

Accounts
Receivable

SEE ALSO

For more information about working with asset accounts, see pages 88–89.

Set Up an Accounts Receivable Account

1 Click Accounts on the navigation bar once or twice to display the Account Manager window.

2 Click the New Account button.

3 Leave the Bank Or Financial Institution field empty, and click Next.

4 Select Asset from the list, and click Next.

5 Enter a name for the account so that you can recognize it as your accounts receivable account. You could name it simply "Accounts Receivable," for example. Click Next.

6 Enter zero in the What Is The Value Of This Asset field.

7 Click Next.

8 When Money asks if you want to associate a loan account with the asset, select the No option and click Finish.

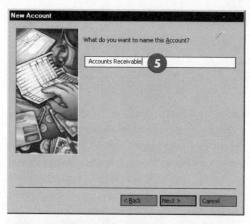

New Account

What do you want to name this Account?

Accounts Receivable **5**

< Back   Next >   Cancel

New Account

Enter the ending balance from your last statement. If you want to start your record keeping from an earlier date, enter the ending balance from the earlier statement, and then enter all transactions from that statement until now.

Note: If you want to track this account from the day you opened it, enter zero. If you don't know your current balance, enter an estimate. You can change it later before you balance the account.

What is the value of this asset?

0.00 **6**

What is the currency for this account?

US Dollar **7**

< Back   Next >   Cancel

Cash-Basis vs. Accrual-Basis Accounting

Cash-basis accounting counts any checking account deposit as income and any checking account withdrawal as an expense. Cash-basis accounting is commonly employed in small businesses because it's easy to use. But it's usually less accurate than the alternative, accrual-basis accounting, in the way that it measures profits. Accrual-basis accounting counts income when you bill customers and counts expense when you charge or incur bills. The problem with accrual-basis accounting, however, is that to use it, you need to understand double-entry bookkeeping.

Cash-basis accounting counts income when you receive the cash and counts expense when you pay a bill. This might sound correct, but it tends to produce some funny profit measurements. For example, if you're using cash-basis accounting to measure your profits, your profits increase when you delay payment of your bills. And if you're using cash-basis accounting and a customer's check arrives next month instead of this month, your profits for the current month decrease. For example, you can easily increase or decrease your records of profits for the year by simply waiting until January 1st to write a check for something purchased during December, or to enter a deposit for a service rendered during December. Accrual-basis accounting counts income when you bill the customer and counts expense when you charge some amount or incur some expense. Accrual-basis accounting more accurately measures your profits in a given time period, but it's more complicated and more work because you use double-entry bookkeeping. All large companies and most small companies use accrual basis accounting because it is less susceptible to manipulation and is employed by all auditors and certified public accountants.

11

Recording an Invoice

How you record an invoice depends on the accounting system you use. If you want to use cash-basis accounting, you simply use your accounts receivable account to list your unpaid invoices. If you use accrual-basis accounting, you record an invoice as an increase in the accounts receivable account, and then you record the payment as a transfer from the accounts receivable account to the bank account.

Record an Invoice with Cash-Basis Accounting

1. Display the accounts receivable account.

2. Click the Increase tab, and if necessary, click New.

3. Enter the invoice date.

4. Enter the name of the customer.

5. Enter the invoice amount.

6. Leave the Category fields empty.

7. Optionally, enter a description of the invoice; for example, a purchase order number.

8. Click Enter.

SEE ALSO

For more information about setting up business income and expense categories, see page 156.

Record an Invoice with Accrual-Basis Accounting

1 Display the accounts receivable account.

2 Click the Increase tab, and if necessary, click New.

3 Enter the invoice date.

4 Enter the name of the customer.

5 Enter the invoice amount.

6 Use the Category fields to specify an income category. By doing this, you count a customer invoice as income when you bill rather than when you collect.

7 Optionally, enter a description of the invoice; for example, a purchase order number.

8 Click Enter.

11

Recording a Customer Payment

How you record a customer payment depends on the accounting system you use. To record a customer payment using cash-basis accounting, you first record the customer's check as a deposit in the bank account and then you record the decrease in the accounts receivable account. To record a customer payment using accrual-basis accounting, you record a deposit in the bank account and transfer the money from the accounts receivable account.

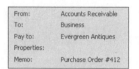

From:	Accounts Receivable
To:	Business
Pay to:	Evergreen Antiques
Properties:	
Memo:	Purchase Order #412

> **TIP**
>
> *Don't forget to record and categorize the customer's check in the business account's register. For more information on how to do this, see page 158.*

Record a Customer Payment with Cash-Basis Accounting

1. Display the accounts receivable account's register.

2. Click the Decrease tab, and if necessary, click New.

3. Enter the payment date.

4. Select the customer's name from the Pay To field.

5. Enter the amount of the check.

6. Leave the Category fields empty.

7. Optionally, enter a description of the check, such as the customer's check number, in the Memo field.

8. Click Enter.

9. Mark the invoice(s) that the customer's check pays and the customer's check as reconciled by right-clicking each transaction and choosing the shortcut menu's Mark As command and the Mark As submenu's Reconciled command.

TIP

To mark the invoices that the customer's check pays as reconciled, display the accounts receivable account register and right-click the invoice transaction. Then choose the shortcut menu's Mark As Command and the Mark As Submenu's Reconciled Command. Repeat this process for the transfer transaction to mark it as reconciled as well.

Record a Customer Payment with Accrual-Basis Accounting

1 Display the business' bank account register.

2 Click the Deposit tab, and if necessary, click New.

3 Enter the customer's check number.

4 Enter the payment date.

5 Click the down arrow in the From field, and select the name of the customer making the payment.

6 Enter the amount of the check.

7 Enter Transfer in the Category field.

8 Click the down arrow in the Subcategory field, and select the name of the accounts receivable account.

9 Optionally, enter a memo describing of the check.

10 Click Enter.

11

Monitoring Accounts Receivable

On a regular basis, you need to review your accounts receivable. In particular, you want to watch out for delinquent customer invoices—invoices that should have been paid but haven't been paid. To do this, you can produce a report that summarizes the transactions in the accounts receivable account and sorts the information by customer name.

[🗐 Account Transactions]

Produce an Accounts Receivable Report

1 Click Reports on the navigation bar.

2 Click Spending Habits on the Reports & Charts bar.

3 Select Account Transactions from the list.

4 Click the Go To Report/ Chart button.

5 Click Customize on the Accounts bar.

6 Specify which pieces of register information you want to appear on the report. If you aren't using the Category fields when you enter transactions, you can clear the Categories box, for instance. If you are using the Memo field to store information such as invoice numbers or check numbers, you should make sure the Memo box is checked.

7 Click the down arrow in the From Account field, and select your accounts receivable account.

8 Click the Select Transactions option button to display the Select Transactions dialog box.

TIP

If you're using cash-basis accounting, you can clear the Category check box.

9 Click the Details tab.

10 Select Unreconciled Transactions from the Status field.

11 Click OK.

12 Select Payees from the Subtotal By field.

13 Click View to update the Account Transactions report so that it summarizes the invoices and payments by customer.

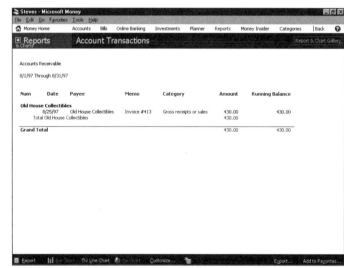

Setting Up Payroll Accounts to Track Withholdings

Money doesn't provide a payroll feature as such, but it can dramatically reduce the work of preparing a payroll. You can use Money, for example, to record and print payroll checks. You can also produce quarterly and yearly payroll reports that you can use to prepare payroll tax returns. The first thing you need to do to begin tracking payroll expenses using Money is to set up payroll liability accounts. Specifically, you need liability accounts to track Social Security taxes, Medicare taxes, and federal income tax withholdings.

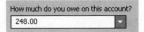

Set Up Payroll Liability Accounts

1 Click Accounts on the navigation bar once or twice to display the Account Manager window.

2 Click the New Account button to start the New Account wizard.

3 Leave the Bank Or Financial Institution field empty, and click Next.

4 Select Liability from the list of account types, and click Next.

5 Enter a name for the liability account. For example, use the names Social Security, Medicare, and Federal Income to track the different taxes you withhold and owe. Click Next.

6 Enter the amount you currently owe for the tax, and click Finish.

7 Repeat steps 2 through 6 to set up a separate account for each of the taxes.

Payroll Tax Reporting Requirements

To meet the federal payroll tax and reporting requirements, your first step is to get an employer tax identification number. This number is equivalent to your personal Social Security number—it identifies you as an employer and is used by the government to track transactions relating specifically to your responsibilities as an employer. To get an employer tax identification number, contact the Internal Revenue Service and ask for an SS-4 form. This form, which is very simple to fill out, tells the IRS you want to hire an employee.

Once you request an employer tax identification number, the IRS knows you're an employer and sends you the federal tax deposit coupons you use to remit the money withheld from employees' paychecks. And, at the end of the quarter and the end of the year, the IRS sends you the payroll tax returns you need to complete: the end-of-quarter 941 return to report the wages you've paid for the quarter and the end-of-year 940 return to report any federal unemployment tax you owe.

The IRS also sends you a copy of the *Employer's Tax Guide*. This booklet, which is sometimes called a "Circular E," tells you how much federal income tax, Social Security tax, and Medicare tax you're supposed to withhold from an employee's paycheck. You need this booklet to prepare payroll checks. Watch for it, and don't lose it.

State and Local Payroll Tax and Reporting Requirements

Your state also has payroll tax and reporting requirements that you need to meet. States, for example, require employers to pay unemployment insurance and disability insurance, also known as "workman's compensation." Most states have a state income tax that you, as an employer, need to withhold from employee checks and then remit to the state. You may also have local county or city payroll tax reporting requirements.

I can't give you precise instructions for meeting state and local payroll tax reporting requirements because they vary from state to state. Contact the state or local employment tax office, and tell them you are hiring an employee or several employees. The office will put you on its list of employers. Typically, as soon as this happens, you get instructions on what you're supposed to do. And you periodically get payroll tax returns you're supposed to fill out and return. (End-of-quarter payroll tax returns are common, for example.)

Other Employee Reporting Requirements

Let me mention one other item related to all this. In addition to the payroll tax and reporting requirements described in the preceding paragraphs, employers are also required to perform other tasks. The Immigration and Naturalization Service, for example, requires employers to verify that their employees are U.S. citizens, Permanent Residents, or have a work visa. Some states have special reporting requirements, for example, to help track down parents who aren't making court-ordered child support payments. And there are often other special reporting requirements as well.

11

Setting Up Payroll Categories

Once you've set up your payroll liability accounts, you need to set up several new payroll expense categories. Specifically, you need to set up a category called Payroll and several subcategories within this category to track your taxes and payroll expenses.

SEE ALSO

For more information on assigning categories a line on a particular tax form, see pages 82–83.

Set Up the Payroll Expense Category

1 Click Categories on the navigation bar.

2 Click the New button.

3 Click the Create A New Category option button, and click Next.

4 Enter the new category name as Payroll in the Name field.

5 Click the Expense option button, and click Next.

6 Select Other Expense from the list.

7 Click Finish.

New Category

Categorizing your income and expenses accurately helps Money give you useful information about your financial situation. Money needs information about this new category in order to create it.

First, give this new category a descriptive name so you can easily identify it later.

Name: Payroll **4**

Category type
○ Income
◉ Expense **5**

< Back | Next > | Cancel

Set Up Payroll Expense Subcategories

1 Click Categories on the navigation bar.

2 Select Payroll from the Categories field.

3 Click New.

4 Click the Add A Subcategory To Payroll option button, and click Next.

5 Enter a name for the new category in the Name field. For example, use the name Gross Wages to track gross wages. Click Next.

6 Click Finish.

7 Repeat steps 3 through 6 to add the other payroll subcategories.

Writing Payroll Checks

Once you've set up the payroll accounts and payroll categories you need, preparing a payroll check is a snap. You just need to figure out how much you're supposed to withhold for the employee based on the information the employee provided on his or her W-4 form and the tables listed in the current Circular E Employer's Tax Guide. Then you enter the amounts you calculate in the Split Transaction dialog box.

Record a Check to an Employee

1 Display the business bank account's register.

2 Click the Check tab, and if necessary, click New.

3 Describe the gross wages on the first line of the Split Transaction dialog box by specifying the Category as Payroll and the Subcategory as Gross Wages. Enter the gross wages in the Amount field.

4 Describe the federal income taxes withheld from the paycheck on the second line by specifying the Category as Transfer and the Subcategory as Federal Income. Enter the amount in the Amount field.

5 Describe the Social Security taxes paid by the employee through withholding on the third line by specifying the Category as Transfer and the Subcategory as Social Security. Enter the amount in the Amount field.

6 Describe the Medicare taxes paid by the employee through withholding on the fourth line by specifying the Category as Transfer and the Subcategory as Medicare. Enter the amount in the Amount field.

Click the Split button.

Click Enter to record the payroll check.

Enter the name of the employee.

Enter the payroll check date.

Enter the payroll check number.

7 Record the Employer's matching Social Security expense on the fifth line by specifying the Category as Payroll and the Subcategory as Employer's Social Security. Enter the amount in the Amount field.

8 Record the amount of money owed the federal government for Social Security tax on the sixth line by specifying the Category as Transfer and the Subcategory as Social Security. Enter the amount in the Amount field.

9 Record the employer's matching Medicare taxes on the seventh line by specifying the Category as Payroll and the Subcategory as Employer's Medicare. Enter the amount in the Amount field.

10 Record the amount of money owed the federal government for this Medicare tax on the eighth line by specifying the Category as Transfer and the Subcategory as Medicare. Enter the amount in the Amount field.

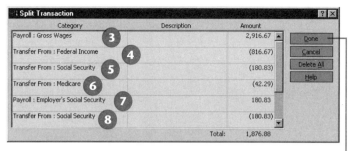

Click Done to close the Split Transaction dialog box.

Preparing W-2 and W-3 Forms

The other payroll task you must complete is the annual preparation of W-2 forms and the W-3 form. You complete a W-2 for each employee to summarize the gross pay earned over the year and the taxes withheld over the year. The W-3 summarizes all the W-2s. Although Money won't print these forms for you, you can use it to calculate the needed information and display it in a report.

Produce a Payroll Transaction Report

1. Click Reports on the navigation bar.

2. Click Spending Habits on the Reports & Charts bar.

3. Select Who Is Getting My Money from the Spending Habits list.

4. Click the Go to Report/ Chart button.

5. Click Customize on the Reports & Charts bar.

6. Change the report's title by clicking the Title field and typing *Employee Wages Summary*.

7. Click the down arrow in the Rows field, and select Subcategories from the list.

8. Click the down arrow in the Columns field, and select Payees from the list.

9. Use the Date Range options to tell Money for which year you want to prepare the W-2s and W-3.

10. Click the Select Transactions option button to display the Select Transactions dialog box.

SEE ALSO

For more information on printing reports, see pages 60–61.

TIP

If Money initially displays a chart instead of a report, click Report.

11 Click the Categories tab.

12 Click the Selected Categories option button.

13 Select the Payroll expense category and the Payroll subcategories from the list, and click OK.

14 Click View to produce the Employee Wages Summary report.

15 Print the report by choosing the File menu's Print command.

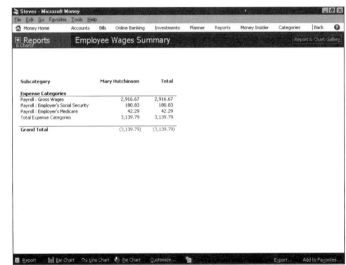

Measuring Profits

There are many reasons for owning or operating a small business. Autonomy, for one, or maybe just plain fun. But for a business to survive, the business must produce profits. Accordingly, on a regular basis, you need to calculate whether or not you're making a profit. As long as you've been collecting information about your income and expenses, it is very easy to produce a Profit and Loss Statement using Money.

Produce a Profit and Loss Statement

1. Click Reports on the navigation bar.

2. Click Spending Habits on the Reports & Charts bar.

3. Select Income vs. Spending from the Spending Habits list.

4. Click the Go To Report/ Chart button.

5. Click Customize.

6. Change the report's title by clicking the Title field, and typing *Profit and Loss Statement*.

7. Use the Date Range options to tell Money for which time period you want to measure profits.

8. Click the Select Transactions option button to display the Select Transactions dialog box.

TIP

The Dates field provides several common profit reporting periods. As a general rule, you want to measure profits on a monthly and an annual basis.

TIP

Getting information on your competitors' profits.
Both Robert Morris & Associates and Standard and Poor's publish financial statistics on a variety of businesses. The data is arranged by size of business and by standard industry classification, or SIC, codes. You can obtain these publications at your local library.

SEE ALSO

For more information about creating and customizing charts, see page 52.

9 Click the Categories tab.

10 Click the Selected Categories option button.

11 Select the business income and expense categories that you want to appear on your Profit and Loss Statement from the list.

12 Click OK.

13 Click View to produce the Profit and Loss Statement.

14 Print the statement by choosing the File menu's Print command.

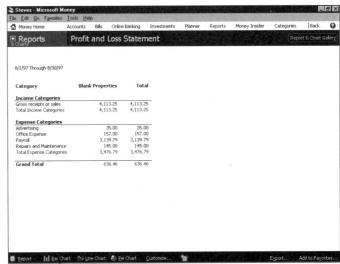

To view your Profit and Loss Statement in a bar chart, click Bar Chart.

Measuring Cash Flow

Over the long haul, a business can't survive without profits, but cash flow is more important in the short run. To make it through the next month or quarter, for example, you need to have enough cash to pay all your bills and to make any needed investments in new machinery or equipment.

Produce a Monthly Cash Flow Statement

1 Click Reports on the navigation bar.

2 Click Spending Habits on the Reports & Charts bar.

3 Select Monthly Cash Flow from the Spending Habits list.

4 Click the Go To Report/ Chart button.

5 Click Customize.

6 Use the Date Range options to tell Money for which time period you want to measure cash flow.

7 Make sure the Include Transfers To Or From Asset Or Liability Accounts option button is selected.

8 Click the Select Transactions option button.

Why does my cash flow differ from my profit? *If you record your business income when you deposit customer payments and you record your business expenses when you write checks, you use cash-basis accounting. In this case, your profit and loss statement will closely resemble your cash-flow statement. The only differences will result from account transfers to and from your bank accounts. These transfers appear on cash-flow statements because they involve cash moving in or out of a bank account. But they don't appear on profit and loss statements.*

9 Click the Categories tab.

10 Click the Selected Categories option button.

11 Select the business income and expense categories that you want to appear on your Cash Flow Statement from the list.

12 Click OK.

13 Click View to produce the Cash Flow Statement.

14 Print the statement by choosing the File menu's Print command.

To view your Cash Flow Statement in a bar chart, click Bar Chart.

Measuring Net Worth

With a balance sheet, you tally your assets and liabilities and calculate the difference between these two amounts to get your business's net worth. A balance sheet provides several pieces of useful information. It lets you assess the liquidity of your business, helps you calculate return on investment figures, and provides information you need to determine how fast you can grow your business.

Produce a Balance Sheet

1. Click Reports on the navigation bar.

2. Click What I Have on the Reports & Charts bar.

3. Select Account Balances from the What I Have list.

4. Click the Go To Report/ Chart button.

5. Click the Customize button.

6. Change the report's title by clicking in the Title field and typing *Balance Sheet*.

7. Use the Show Balances As Of field to specify the date for which you want the account balance calculated.

8. Click the down arrow in the Accounts field, and select Multiple Accounts from the list.

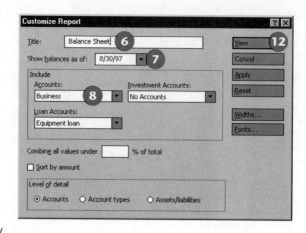

How fast can I grow my business? *In general, you can grow your business only as fast as you can grow your net worth. For example, if you want to grow your business by 25 percent annually, you need to grow your net worth by 25 percent annually. Because a small business usually increases its net worth only by reinvesting profits, however, these reinvested profits limit your growth. For example, if reinvested profits as a percentage of net worth equal 20 percent, you can only grow your business by 20 percent.*

Interpreting the Balance Sheet. *A general rule of thumb is that the sum of your cash, accounts receivable, and any investments should at least be equal to your short-term debts. Your short-term debts include liabilities you have to pay in the coming year, any amounts you now owe employees or creditors, business credit-card balances, and the loan principal payments you'll make over the next year. You should be able to get all of this information from your Balance Sheet.*

9 Click the Selected Accounts option button.

10 Select the business account that you want to appear on your Balance Sheet from the list.

11 Click OK.

12 Click View to produce the Balance Sheet.

13 Print the Balance Sheet by choosing the File menu's Print command.

Index

checks
 printing, 32–33
 splitting transactions, 26
 voiding, 27
 writing payroll checks,
  172–73
children
 Microsoft Money files for, 9
 saving for their college
  expenses, 74–77
classification, property, 129
closing accounts, 38
college
 calculating how much to
  save, 74–75
 financial aid, 77, 79
 investing savings, 76
 planning for, 74–79
 tips for reducing cost, 78–79
column widths, changing, 58
comments
 adding to account information, 18
 adding to transactions, 24
consumer credit, 85
credit cards
 benefits of tracking in Money,
  39
 and Debt Reduction Planner,
  45
 reconciling accounts, 46–47
 recording credits, 43
 recording payments, 44
 recording purchases, 42
 reducing use, 69
 setting up Money accounts,
  40–41
Currency Converter, 23
customer payments, recording,
 154–65

dates
 entering, 24
 searching for transactions
  by, 31
 selecting for reports, 56
Debt Reduction Planner, 45
deductions, paycheck, 20–21
deductions, tax
 bunching, 84–85
 recordkeeping, 82–83
 taking, 84
defined benefit plans, 72–73
deleting
 accounts, 38
 transactions, 27
deposits
 recording, 19
 recurring, 29
depreciation, 130, 131
distributions, recording, 110
dividends
 recording, 110
 reinvesting, 111

electronic payments
 automatic, 142–45
 canceling a payment, 141
 checking status, 141
 entering, 138–39
 sending, 140
 setting up online services,
  136–37
e-mail, sending to banks, 149
employer pension plans, 72–73

errors
 fixing transaction entries, 27
 in loan account balances, 96
 reconciling bank statements,
  36–37
Excel, exporting Money reports
 to, 63
exchange rates, 23
exiting Microsoft Money, 13
expenses
 categorizing, 22, 156
 recording, 22–23
 recurring, 28
 viewing spending habits, 68–
  69
exporting reports, 63

fictitious transactions, 37
files
 archiving, 12
 backup, 8, 9, 13
 creating, 8
 displaying, 9
 exporting, 63
 importing from Quicken, 9
 location of, 9
 multiple, 9
 naming, 9
 opening, 8
 restoring, 8
 saving, 9, 13
 separate, 9
financial aid, 77, 79
financial planning, 65–85
Financial Suite
 defined, 65

Financial Suite, *continued*

 Home Inventory
  Worksheet, 91
 Home Worksheet, 97
 Loan Worksheet, 100
 Planner, 45, 65, 66, 67, 70–
  71, 74–75, 77, 80–81
 Tax Estimator, 83
finding
 help topics, 11
 transactions, 30–31
fixing errors, 27
fonts, changing, 59
forgotten transactions, 37
formatting reports, 58–59
401(k) plans, 85

graphs. *See* charts

help, online, 11
home. *See also* mortgages
 calculating loan payments, 97
 inventorying assets, 90–91
 as real estate investment, 121
 saving money for down
  payment, 80–81
 setting up asset account, 88
 tips for recordkeeping, 90–91
home equity loans, 85
Home Inventory Worksheet, 91
Home screen, 10
Home Worksheet, 97

retirement, *continued*

steps in planning, 72–73
tax-deferred savings, 85
return of capital
defined, 114
recording transactions, 126

saving files, 9, 13
savings
calculating college needs,
74–79
calculating retirement needs,
70–71
investing college savings, 76
for major purchases, 80
Schedule C, list of categories,
157
searching
for help topics, 11
for transactions, 30–31
SEP/IRAs, 85
Set Lifetime Goals & Events
button, 70, 80
short-term debts, 181
small business
accounts receivable, 160,
166–67
balance sheets, 180–81
cash flow statements, 178–79
competitor data, 177
measuring net worth, 180–81
payroll, 168–74
profit and loss statements,
176–77
recording customer pay-
ments, 164–65

small business, *continued*

recording expenses, 159
recording income, 158
recording invoices, 162–63
Spending Habits reports, 51, 54,
67, 134
splits, stock, 113
splitting transactions, 26
starting Microsoft Money, 7
state and local taxes, reporting
requirements, 169
stocks
average annual return, 71
for college savings, 76
obtaining quotes online, 150–
51
recording distributions, 110
recording dividends, 110
recording purchases, 108
recording sales, 109
recording splits, 113
reinvesting dividends, 111
stock splits, 113
stock symbols, 150

tab-delimited text files,
exporting Money reports
as, 63
tax-deferred accounts, tracking,
102
taxes
list of Schedule C categories,
157
payroll reporting requirements, 169

taxes, *continued*

tax-related Money categories,
82–83, 157, 171
tax-related reports, 51, 54, 55
tips for saving on, 84–85
tracking deductions, 82–83
Tax Estimator, 83
Tell Money About Yourself
button, 66
text files, exporting Money
reports as, 63
transaction forms, 19, 24
transactions. *See also* account
register
deleting, 27
editing, 27
fictitious, 37
finding, 30–31
forgotten, 37
lost, 30–31
recurring, 28–29
splitting, 26
tips for entering, 24
transfers, recording, 25
tuition, college. *See* college
.txt files, 63

U.S. savings bonds, tracking,
103

voiding checks, 27

Wall Street Journal, 153
weddings, saving for, 80–81
W-2 forms, 172–73
W-3 forms, 172–73
What I Have reports, 51
What I Owe reports, 51
withholding, 83, 168
worksheets, 91, 97, 100
World Wide Web, 153

year-end reports, 54, 55

zero-coupon bonds, 114

The manuscript for this book was prepared and submitted to Microsoft Press in electronic form. Text files were prepared using Microsoft Word 97. Pages were composed by Stephen L. Nelson, Inc. using PageMaker for Windows, with text in Stone Sans and display type in Stone Serif and Stone Serif Semibold. Composed pages were delivered to the printer as electronic prepress files.

Cover Designer

Tim Girvin Design

Interior Graphic Designer

designLab

Kim Eggleston

Graphic Layout

Stefan Knorr

Indexer

Julie Kawabata

Things are looking up!

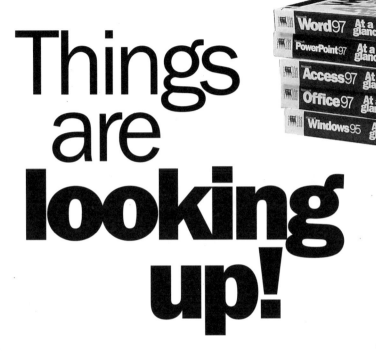

Here's the remarkable, *visual* way to quickly find answers about Microsoft applications and operating systems. Microsoft Press® *At a Glance* books let you focus on particular tasks and show you with clear, numbered steps the easiest way to get them done right now.

Microsoft Press® products are available worldwide wherever quality computer books are sold. For more information, contact your book or computer retailer, software reseller, or local Microsoft Sales Office, or visit our Web site at mspress.microsoft.com. To locate your nearest source for Microsoft Press products, or to order directly, call 1-800-MSPRESS in the U.S. (in Canada, call 1-800-268-2222).

Prices and availability dates are subject to change.

Get quick, easy answers— anywhere!

Microsoft Press® Field Guides are a quick, accurate source of information about Microsoft Office 97 applications. In no time, you'll have the lay of the land, identify toolbar buttons and commands, stay safely out of danger, and have all the tools you need for survival!

Microsoft® Excel 97 Field Guide
Stephen L. Nelson
U.S.A. $9.95   ($12.95 Canada)
ISBN 1-57231-326-9

Microsoft® Word 97 Field Guide
Stephen L. Nelson
U.S.A. $9.95   ($12.95 Canada)
ISBN 1-57231-325-0

Microsoft® PowerPoint® 97 Field Guide
Stephen L. Nelson
U.S.A. $9.95   ($12.95 Canada)
ISBN 1-57231-327-7

Microsoft® Outlook™ 97 Field Guide
Stephen L. Nelson
U.S.A. $9.99   ($12.99 Canada)
ISBN 1-57231-383-8

Microsoft® Access 97 Field Guide
Stephen L. Nelson
U.S.A. $9.95   ($12.95 Canada)
ISBN 1-57231-328-5

Microsoft Press® products are available worldwide wherever quality computer books are sold. For more information, contact your book or computer retailer, software reseller, or local Microsoft Sales Office, or visit our Web site at mspress.microsoft.com. To locate your nearest source for Microsoft Press products, or to order directly, call 1-800-MSPRESS in the U.S. (in Canada, call 1-800-268-2222).

Prices and availability dates are subject to change.

Microsoft Press

Keep things **running** smoothly around the **Office.**

These are *the* answer books for business users of Microsoft Office 97 applications. They are packed with everything from quick, clear instructions for new users to comprehensive answers for power users. The Microsoft Press® *Running* series features authoritative handbooks you'll keep by your computer and use every day.

Running Microsoft® Excel 97
Mark Dodge, Chris Kinata, and Craig Stinson
U.S.A. $39.95   ($54.95 Canada)
ISBN 1-57231-321-8

Running Microsoft® Word 97
Russell Borland
U.S.A. $39.95   ($53.95 Canada)
ISBN 1-57231-320-X

Running Microsoft® PowerPoint® 97
Stephen W. Sagman
U.S.A. $29.95   ($39.95 Canada)
ISBN 1-57231-324-2

Running Microsoft® Access 97
John Viescas
U.S.A. $39.95   ($54.95 Canada)
ISBN 1-57231-323-4

Running Microsoft® Office 97
Michael Halvorson and Michael Young
U.S.A. $39.95   ($53.95 Canada)
ISBN 1-57231-322-6

Microsoft®*Press*

Take productivity in stride.

Microsoft Press® *Step by Step* books provide quick and easy self-paced training that will help you learn to use the powerful word processor, spreadsheet, database, desktop information manager, and presentation applications of Microsoft Office 97, both individually and together. Prepared by the professional trainers at Catapult, Inc. and Perspection, Inc., these books present easy-to-follow lessons with clear objectives, real-world business examples, and numerous screen shots and illustrations. Each book contains approximately eight hours of instruction. Put Microsoft's Office 97 applications to work today, *Step by Step*.

Microsoft® Excel 97 Step by Step
U.S.A. $29.95   ($39.95 Canada)
ISBN 1-57231-314-5

Microsoft® Word 97 Step by Step
U.S.A. $29.95   ($39.95 Canada)
ISBN 1-57231-313-7

Microsoft® PowerPoint® 97
 Step by Step
U.S.A. $29.95   ($39.95 Canada)
ISBN 1-57231-315-3

Microsoft® Outlook™ 97 Step by Step
U.S.A. $29.99   ($39.99 Canada)
ISBN 1-57231-382-X

Microsoft® Access 97 Step by Step
U.S.A. $29.95   ($39.95 Canada)
ISBN 1-57231-316-1

Microsoft® Office 97 Integration
 Step by Step
U.S.A. $29.95   ($39.95 Canada)
ISBN 1-57231-317-X

Microsoft Press® products are available worldwide wherever quality computer books are sold. For more information, contact your book or computer retailer, software reseller, or local Microsoft Sales Office, or visit our Web site at mspress.microsoft.com. To locate your nearest source for Microsoft Press products, or to order directly, call 1-800-MSPRESS in the U.S. (in Canada, call 1-800-268-2222).

Prices and availability dates are subject to change.

Microsoft Press

Register Today!

Return this
Microsoft® Money 98 At a Glance
registration card for
a Microsoft Press® catalog

U.S. and Canada addresses only. Fill in information below and mail postage-free. Please mail only the bottom half of this page.

1-57231-639-XA   **MICROSOFT® MONEY 98**   *Owner Registration Card*
                                AT A GLANCE

NAME

INSTITUTION OR COMPANY NAME

ADDRESS

CITY   STATE   ZIP

Microsoft®*Press*
Quality Computer Books

**For a free catalog of
Microsoft Press® products, call
1-800-MSPRESS**

BUSINESS REPLY MAIL
FIRST-CLASS MAIL   PERMIT NO. 53   BOTHELL, WA

POSTAGE WILL BE PAID BY ADDRESSEE

NO POSTAGE
NECESSARY
IF MAILED
IN THE
UNITED STATES

MICROSOFT PRESS REGISTRATION
MICROSOFT® MONEY 98 AT A GLANCE
PO BOX 3019
BOTHELL   WA   98041-9946